COMMENTARY ON THE PILGRIM'S PROGRESS.

CHRISTIANA AND FAMILY SET OUT.

COMMENTARY

ON

JOHN BUNYAN'S

THE PILGRIM'S PROGRESS

FROM THIS WORLD TO THAT WHICH IS TO COME: DELIVERED UNDER THE SIMILITUDE OF A DREAM WHEREIN IS DISCOVERED, THE MANNER OF HIS SETTING OUT, HIS DANGEROUS JOURNEY; AND SAFE ARRIVAL AT THE DESIRED COUNTREY.

BY

REV. ROBERT MAGUIRE, M. A.

COMPILED BY
CHARLES J. DOE.

A PUBLICATION OF

MINNEAPOLIS,
2009

Published by Curiosmith.
P. O. Box 390293, Minneapolis, Minnesota, 55439.
Internet: curiosmith.com.
E-mail: shopkeeper@curiosmith.com.

Scripture quotations are from the *Holy Bible*, King James Version.

All footnotes are added by the publisher.

Compilation, supplementary content, and cover design:
Copyright © 2009 Charles J. Doe.

ISBN 978-0-9817505-8-3

Library of Congress Control Number: 2009940007

CONTENTS.

PART I.

I.	THE DEN AND THE DREAMER	9
II.	THE SLOUGH OF DESPOND	14
III.	WORLDLY-WISEMAN.	19
IV.	THE WICKET-GATE.	26
V.	THE INTERPRETER'S HOUSE	29
VI.	THE CROSS AND THE CONTRAST	37
VII.	THE HILL DIFFICULTY	42
VIII.	THE PALACE BEAUTIFUL	46
IX.	APOLLYON	56
X.	THE VALLEY OF THE SHADOW OF DEATH	60
XI.	CHRISTIAN AND FAITHFUL.	65
XII.	TALKATIVE	71
XIII.	VANITY FAIR	77
XIV.	CHRISTIAN AND HOPEFUL.	84
XV.	DOUBTING CASTLE AND GIANT DESPAIR	90
XVI.	THE DELECTABLE MOUNTAINS	97
XVII.	THE ENCHANTED GROUND	101
XVIII.	IGNORANCE	111
XIX.	THE LAND OF BEULAH	117

CONTENTS.

PART II.

I.	CHRISTIANA	123
II.	THE WICKET-GATE	128
III.	THE INTERPRETER'S HOUSE.	133
IV.	THE CROSS AND THE CONSEQUENCES.	137
V.	THE PALACE BEAUTIFUL	142
VI.	THE VALLEY OF HUMILIATION	149
VII.	MR. HONEST AND MR. FEARING.	154
VIII.	THE GUESTS OF GAIUS.	160
IX.	VANITY FAIR AND MR. MNASON'S HOUSE.	167
X.	THE DELECTABLE MOUNTAINS AND THE SHEPHERDS	171
XI.	MR. VALIANT-FOR-TRUTH	176
XII.	THE ENCHANTED GROUND	180
XIII.	THE PILGRIMS AT HOME.	184

PUBLISHER'S NOTE.

The notes of Rev. Robert Maguire were compiled from the footnotes of John Bunyan's *The Pilgrim's Progress*, an edition published by Cassell, Petter, and Galpin, c. 1863. Each chapter begins with an introduction which is followed by notes, comments and symbolic meanings. All notes are maintained in the same chapter and same order they appeared. Many of the poems interspersed throughout the text were written by Robert Maguire.

CHAPTER I.

THE DEN AND THE DREAMER.

INTRODUCTION.—"His is the highest miracle of genius," says Lord Macaulay, "that the imaginations of one mind should become the personal recollections of another: and this miracle the tinker has wrought. There is no ascent, no declivity, no resting-place, no turnstile, with which we are not perfectly acquainted." This is well said; and it is true. The PILGRIM'S PROGRESS is one of the best known books of human origin. It is a household book. Men love to retrace the steps of the journey, to re-visit the familiar scenes of the wondrous Pilgrimage, and to live over again the experiences of the Pilgrim.

The Dreamer rests himself in his dreary prison-house, and as he sleeps, he sees the outline of a Vision. And whether it be in his sleeping or his waking moments, 'tis true that Heaven hath somehow drawn aside the veil, and revealed these grand and glorious sights which reach so near to the things that "eye hath not seen," permitting this far-sighted man to look

"Through golden vistas into Heaven."*

The opening of the Vision presents in bold relief the future hero of the allegory—a burdened man, clothed with rags; weeping because of threatened woe, pronounced by the Book that is in his hand. He dwells in the CITY OF DESTRUCTION. He reveals his sorrows and anxieties to his wife and family, but finds no sympathy there; and failing to obtain companionship on the heavenward road, he starts alone upon this spiritual journey. Here he by-and-by meets EVANGELIST, and is by him directed to flee *from* the wrath to come, and to flee *to* the Wicket-gate beyond. While pursuing his onward path, he is overtaken by two of his neighbors, OBSTINATE and PLIABLE, who seek to turn him away from his purpose, and to fetch him back by force. CHRISTIAN (for that is his name) refuses to return; whereupon OBSTINATE turns back, but PLIABLE determines to try the fortune of the way, having an idea that throughout it is naught else but sunshine. CHRISTIAN is led by principle; while PLIABLE is urged on only by impulse.

---

*Thomas Moore, "Thou Art, O God."

The wilderness of this world.—The world is a wilderness to the Christian. He is not at home; dwells in tents; has only sandy foundations for all his earthly things. Therefore is the Christian man a pilgrim. With the pilgrim's tottering staff, and with the pilgrim's scanty fare, he is ever looking upward, going forward, tending onward, wayworn, weather-beaten, houseless, homeless—he is now in the wilderness, but the marching pilgrim is ever "nearing home." And as he progresses in his pilgrimage, his hopes grow brighter, and his prospects clearer; his staff is strengthened, and by-and-by it comforteth him. As he climbs the hill, he rises to a more bracing atmosphere; and his strength is proportioned to his need. "As thy days, so shall thy strength be."

Where was a den.—This was the dungeon of the gaol in Bedford, in which Bunyan was imprisoned for conscience' and the Gospel's sake. How God makes the wrath of man to praise him! When the fierce Domitian had banished John to the wild and barren rock of Patmos, then heaven itself opens to his view, and he is commanded to write the words of the Revelation. Jealousy and hatred imprisoned Luther for ten months in the castle of Wartburg; but God made use of the interval by permitting the great Reformer, in this his Patmos, to translate the Scriptures into the tongue of the German nation. And so Bunyan is now withdrawn from the agitation and excitement of the world outside, and in what he calls his "den," he sees visions, and dreams dreams, and indites the wondrous parables and allegories in which, "though dead, he yet speaketh."

And as I slept, I dreamed.—Bunyan, though bereft of liberty in a damp and dreary dungeon, threw his allegory into the likeness of a peaceful dream. Sweet and deep, doubtless, was the sleep of this man of God, conscious that he was undergoing hardship for the cause of Christ, and that nothing worthy of bonds had been proved against him. Blessed are the night visions and mid-day meditations of such a "seer."

And behold I saw a man, etc.—Mark the features of this vision. This man is the personification of the sinner awakened to conscience of his sins. He is "clothed with rags"—the rags of his own righteousness; "standing"—still in doubt, not yet set forward; "his face from his own house"—looking the right way; "a book in his hand"—the Bible; and "a great burden on his back"—the weary burden of his sin; "he wept and trembled," as every man must do that is under conviction of sin.

What shall I do?—This is his first question; and the second is, "What shall I do *to be saved?*" The convicted sinner's first thought is of his danger, as though it would crush him; the next is, of the possibility of escape—salvation.

He brake his mind to his wife.—This paragraph minutely depicts the agony of an awakened sinner—disclosing some threatening evil to those he loves best, and would rescue if he can; those days of weeping, those restless nights, those darksome dawnings of the morning, that bring not joy, but the weary verdict, "Worse and worse."

I saw a man named Evangelist.—Much of Bunyan's private history is interwoven throughout the allegory. In fact, it is a spiritual autobiography, recounting his own dangers, doubts, helps, and manifold experiences. "EVANGELIST" is supposed to mean the good Mr. Gifford, under whose instruction and ministry Bunyan so greatly profited. Mr. Gifford had been a major in the king's army, and a persecutor of those who, like Bunyan, over-stepped the narrow bounds of that unhappy period. He, however, afterwards became a converted man, and was the founder of a church in Bedford, which was subsequently ministered to by Bunyan himself, and has continued its succession of testimony to the present day.

Wherefore dost thou cry?—What a volume might be written in answer to this question! Everything conspires to draw forth his sighs and tears. The weight of his burden; the lack of sympathy at home; the derision, the chiding, the neglect which he received from friends; the musing upon his forlorn condition in the secrecy of his chamber, and in his solitary walks; the dread realization of sin, and fear of death, and conscious unpreparedness for judgment—all these circumstances conspire to open the fountain of his tears.

Prison—judgment—execution.—This progression of wrath and condemnation, arising out of conviction of sin, alarms the Pilgrim. He sees scope beyond scope, depth beyond depth, darkness beyond darkness; and being as yet without hope and without God in the world, he sees no light at all to illuminate this darksome prospect.

He fears the "prison," the first stage of spiritual apprehension, into which he enters for trial; and seeing he enters that prison with a conscience deeply convicted of guilt and sin, and knowing how unerring is the mind of God, and how stern and unbending is the justice of his throne, that prison becomes the inevitable threshold to "judgment."

He is still more terribly afraid of "judgment." There is no plea of innocence; there is no extenuation of his sin; there is nothing in himself to mitigate the wrath, or to turn aside the judgment of God. To him, then, judgment is the proof of his guilt, and the consequent sentence of death is pronounced against him. And this involves a yet further sequel—"execution."

And most of all he fears this doom of "execution." He is brought by conviction of sin into prison; and from prison to judgment; and from judgment to execution; and that is, not only death, but something after death; not only the grave, but something "lower than the grave;"—it is death, of body and of soul, loss of life and loss of heaven, and all the eternity of woe, and all the unutterable misery that is wrapped up in the doom of the lost and in the destiny of hell.

A parchment roll.—This was Evangelist's gift to the Pilgrim, with a motto that urged him to flight. And this was quickly followed by the further counsel, whither to flee. The roll of parchment, as on other occasions, means that the advice of Evangelist is to be retained and preserved as an enduring possession. Now there is hope!

Yonder wicket-gate.—Not yet attained; yet further on. The Pilgrim is short-sighted; he cannot see the gate. It is seen and may be known by its halo of light. Thus Evangelist acts as a finger-post, directing the way, and helping the power of the Pilgrim's eye-sight.

The man began to run.—The directions once given, his earnestness quickens his steps; and whatever doubt or hesitancy may have been before, now at least he can do naught else but *run*. He is on for his life, and must not delay. No, not for wife or child, or the overture of any friend. They are content to remain in sin, and to dwell in the midst of danger and destruction; and this being so, he takes his spiritual way alone. It is, in fact, a family circle, which now presents just one of its members convinced of sin, but all the rest impenitent and unbelieving. This one member would desire to have all the other members to bear him company toward Zion; but they refuse. His mind is made up to go alone, rather than not to go at all. And out of the midst of the threatened overthrow he speeds his onward way, still bearing his family company in temporal things, but in things spiritual he is all alone.

How often does it happen that one member of a family starts for heaven without father, or mother, or brother, or sister, to bear him company! It is this that divides and separates families and friendships here; and if they become not one in Christ it separates eternally hereafter. Many such separate pilgrimages are undertaken even now; the husband without the wife; the wife without the husband. It may be twain brothers, or two fond sisters, alike in disposition and deportment—alike, it may be, in the externals of religion, and yet separated by this dividing line. Like two rivers, rising from the selfsame fountain, and running side by side at the outset of their course, but then, by a slight and gentle deviation, parting company, and at last, in opposite directions, mingling their waters with the ocean: the one amid the verdure and foliage, and fruits and flowers, of the tropics; the other amid the ice-bound regions of perpetual barrenness and desolation.

Obstinate and Pliable.—This personification of abstract terms adds much to the interest of "The Pilgrim's Progress," and lends a great charm to the characters introduced. These two are named from their nature, which soon manifests itself in their conduct.

OBSTINATE is evidently a mocker, who scoffs at the possessors of religion. He cannot understand why the Pilgrim should leave his worldly associations, or believe the book that bids him to forsake all for Christ. He even waxes angry because his words seem to take no effect. And by-and-by he rails on the Pilgrim, and reviles him for what he believes to be his folly or his fancy in committing himself to the fortunes of so strange an expedition.

PLIABLE yields for a time; is easily turned hither and thither; but has no perseverance in the right way. He is caught by promises, and is beckoned on by hopes, but counts not the cost of the journey. He is pliable for good, or he is pliable for evil; and is ready for either way, according to circumstances.

Meanwhile the Pilgrim, who is now for the first time called by the name of CHRISTIAN, is fighting a hard fight, and he is waging it well. He contends in faith and hope. His *faith* leads him to leave friends and comforts behind him, which OBSTINATE will not do. His *hope* points to the glory beyond—the incorruptible inheritance. His Book teaches him all this; the testimony of that Book is confirmed by the blood of Him that gave it; and thus, with the faith that forsakes house, and family, and friends for Christ, and with the hope that beckons on to the better land, CHRISTIAN determines to hold fast by the plough which he hath put his hand unto. Hence this formidable temptation is successfully resisted, and the Pilgrim steadily pursues his way; OBSTINATE turns back, and is got rid of as an enemy, while PLIABLE goes on, and (for a time at least) bears the Pilgrim company as a friend.

CHAPTER II.

THE SLOUGH OF DESPOND.

INTRODUCTION.—OBSTINATE in his self-will has returned to the City of Destruction. PLIABLE, won for a moment to the cause of the Pilgrim, pliably tries the fortune of the road, merely for speculation and experiment. So long as Religion walks in silver sandals and enjoys the sunshine, he is content to abide with CHRISTIAN; but if the sky should darken, or the way prove hazardous he that has turned his face forward will as easily turn backward, and forsake the pilgrimage. The topic of conversation is hopeful and joyous; for they talk about cherubim and seraphim, and the dazzling glories of heaven, and the tearless happiness of the place, and the glittering crowns, and golden harps, and pearly gates of the seat of bliss. All this is permitted, for the contemplation of the promises is the privilege and duty of young beginners, to animate them to a diligent attention to the conditions annexed to the promises. These men looked to future glory and overlooked present duty—their thoughts were fixed on the end of the journey, and they regarded not, as wise men ought to regard, the necessary steps that conduct thereto.

Now, the consequence in their case was that they both fell into the Slough of Despond. They lost sight of the promises contained in God's Holy Word. These are the stepping-stones that, by the good providence of God, are abundantly scattered along the dangerous pass—the ground-work and foot-hold of the pilgrims. We shall see, by-and-by, how useful are these standing points to the feet of pilgrims, when, in the Second Part of the Progress, we view the safe passage of CHRISTIANA and her children over this same unsafe ground. Meanwhile, PLIABLE extricates himself at the side nearest to the City of Destruction. CHRISTIAN, utterly powerless, is delivered by one whose name is HELP.

Made by him that cannot lie.—In answer to PLIABLE'S curious questions, CHRISTIAN refers to his "Book;" and in evidence of the veracity and authority of the Book, he states that "it was made by him that cannot lie." There is no basis of argument, no ground-work of promise, no foot-hold of faith, no certainty at all, unless the Bible be true. To disturb this authority is to destroy fundamental truth; and "if the foundations be destroyed, what shall the righteous do?"

What things are they?—PLIABLE is not very anxious, if anxious at all, about the authority of "the Book." His spirit of curiosity is greater than his spirit of earnest inquiry. He feels no burden, realizes no natural unfitness, and only wants to know what are the hopes held out; and if they be good and profitable, he would desire to have them, if they can be obtained without any self-denial on his part.

And what else?—Still with an insatiable avidity PLIABLE drinks in the descriptions of heaven, and demands yet more. CHRISTIAN is led on by the evident interest he has awakened in the mind of his new comrade. He descants most eloquently of the "endless kingdom," and "everlasting life," and the glorious "garments" of the redeemed. PLIABLE'S pulse beats high; his curiosity is more and more quickened. It is surely something to meet by-and-by with prophets, and apostles, and martyrs, and such company as these.

Are these things to be enjoyed?—"Let us all learn," says a recent writer on the Pilgrim's Progress, "to distinguish an easy *pliable* disposition from the broken heart of a genuine penitent. You may be very opposite to an obstinate man, with whom you have been associated. You may have a great respect for real Christians; but if you confine your view only to the bright side of religion; if you are carried away by its lively representations of peace and rest, and joy and glory, without any thorough awakening to the power and terror of the unseen world, and without any feeling of the burden upon your back—I mean a sense of your depraved and sinful state—if this, I say, be your experience, *your goodness will only be as the morning cloud and the early dew.* You are only a stony-ground hearer. Notwithstanding your lively emotions, your ready profession, your joyful feelings, and your hasty movements, you have no root in yourself. You will endure but for a season. When tribulation or persecution ariseth because of the Word, you will be offended. Oh, the unspeakable blessing of a thoroughly awakened, a deeply humble heart! Let us remember that this is the special work of the Holy Spirit; and however painful or distressing, let us constantly seek, that by his gracious operation it may be actually wrought within us."

Let us mend our pace.—PLIABLE, intent upon the prospective glories of the place, of which he has just received so glowing an account, desires to hasten on. But the Pilgrim, albeit he did hastily run from the City of Destruction, yet now slackens his pace; he can run no longer. PLIABLE feels no weight. He has undertaken, and now thus far continues, his pilgrimage, not by reason of conviction of sin or consciousness of any burden, but because of the glorious prospect of heaven, and the blessedness that CHRISTIAN tells him of. He cannot, therefore, see any reason why he should not run all the way to the possession of these great promises. But the Pilgrim is "weary and heavy laden." Although full of confidence in the words of his Book, which assure him that the kingdom will be freely bestowed on those who sincerely seek it, he is nevertheless weighed down by a sense of sin and so deeply conscious of his own weakness and infirmity, that he cannot step forward thus quickly. For such a race it needs that we "renew our strength;" and they alone can do this who "wait upon the Lord." It is of these that the prophet speaks, "They shall mount up with wings as eagles; they shall run, and not be weary; and they shall walk, and not faint" (Isaiah 40:31). CHRISTIAN knows this, taught by experience to know the weight of his "burden." He therefore checks the presumption of PLIABLE, saying, "I cannot go so fast as I would, by reason of this burden that is on my back."

A very miry slough.—Since CHRISTIAN'S flight from the City of Destruction, this is his first difficulty and downfall—"they being heedless did both fall suddenly into the bog." This was the Slough of Despond. In this miry place CHRISTIAN seems to fare worse than his fellow; for by reason of his burden (that is, conscious sin), he sinks deeper and deeper. PLIABLE, feeling no such burden, is simply bedaubed, but is also most grievously offended. He naturally feels that this *is* a sudden and unlooked-for descent from the crowns, and harps, and dazzling glories of which they had been speaking. Accordingly, having no correct views of the state of man and of the plan of deliverance, in time of temptation or trial he falleth away. PLIABLE'S first experiences offend him; and at once, with a desperate struggle or two, he releases himself from the mire, at that side of the swamp that was nearest his native home.

Not so the Pilgrim of Sion. CHRISTIAN, now left alone, struggles toward the side nearest the Wicket-gate. All-burdened with sin, and sinking in the miry clay, he feels his danger and his desolate condition. How dreary and how dreadful is this place!—

> "Where hardly a human foot could pass,
>   Or a human heart would dare,
> On the quaking turf of the green morass,

His all he had trusted there."*

But CHRISTIAN now looks elsewhere for help, and makes every effort to be free. Some one has well said, "There is one test by which to distinguish the godly from the ungodly, when both have fallen even into the selfsame sin. It is the test by which you may know a sheep from swine, when both have fallen into the same slough, and are, in fact, so bemired that neither by coat nor color can the one be distinguished from the other. How, then, distinguish them? Nothing more easy. The unclean animal, in circumstances agreeable to its nature, wallows in the mire; but the sheep fills the air with its bleating's, nor ceases its struggles to get out."

Thus PLIABLE, disappointed of his hopes, and not being patient of the Pilgrimage, returns to Destruction; while CHRISTIAN, with earnest struggles to be free, still "looks to the hills, from whence cometh his help."

Whose name was Help.—When man has done his best, and yet that best is nothing, then comes HELP. This kind messenger is CHRIST. He reproves the Pilgrim that he had not looked for "the steps." And CHRISTIAN answers that "fear followed" him, and thus he missed the steps. These stepping-stones are the promises of God in Christ. Now "fear" never yet brought a man to the promises; it only drives us from them, so that we lose the way.

Give me thy hand.—Such is the real help that Christ gives the Christian. "His own arm brought salvation." What would have been the condition of any of us had not the hand of the Lord upheld us, as he upheld the affrighted Peter, when his faith failed him, and he began to sink? Hence the Psalmist, after his deliverance, thus tells of the mercy of the Lord: "I waited patiently for the Lord; and he inclined unto me, and heard my cry. He brought me up also out of an horrible pit, out of the miry clay, and set my feet upon a rock, and established my goings. And he hath put a new song in my mouth, even praise unto our God: many shall see it, and fear, and shall trust in the Lord" (Psalm 40:1–3).

Then I stepped to him.—Here the Dreamer takes part in his own vision; that such a swamp as this should be permitted to exist is to him a marvel, and he seeks the interpretation thereof. This, it appears, is the low level of spiritual experience, into which flows the drainage of conviction of sin. Into this Despond most men fall; some to go thence on their Pilgrimage wiser and better men; others, to

---

*Henry Wadsworth Longfellow, "The Slave in the Dismal Swamp."

turn back, and walk no more with Jesus.

Some men whose minds are well instructed in Divine truth, and whose faith in "present help" is lively, do not sink very deeply into this "horrible pit;" while others, whose faith is weak, are almost overwhelmed, and remain for a considerable time with little or no hope. This latter class of persons are commonly those who have gone great lengths in sin, or whose habit it is to brood continually over the evil which they find within their own hearts, instead of looking out of themselves to the Savior, and resting upon those precious words of invitation and encouragement which he addresses to sinners. There is a humility which partakes largely of unbelief, and which, therefore, cannot be a frame of mind pleasing in the sight of God.

And this Slough of Despond continues to the present day, notwithstanding all the efforts that are put forth to mend it, the downfall of many hopeful ones, a grievous snare to many of the Pilgrims of the heavenly way at the commencement of their Christian career. Two hundred years have passed since Bunyan sounded its depths, and it is not mended yet. The whole aggregate influence of the Christian Church and Christian men is insufficient to satisfy its hungry appetite for souls, that sometimes through it go down quick into hell. Instructors, teachers, preachers, guides, missionaries, martyrs, Bibles, churches, all have failed to take effect; the whole working power of Christendom has not succeeded in throwing across this swamp a beaten highway for the Christian to the City of the King. It is only by believing faith in the work of Christ, that this Slough can be safely over-past. "Seek, and ye shall find."

Thus much concerning Pliable.—Such is the career of the unstable professor—weak, impulsive, and vacillating. He sets out with buoyant spirits, and so long as the way is easy and pleasant, he pursues it with alacrity; but when trouble arises and difficulties meet him, he turns aside from Him who alone can help, and following his own devices, falls into a condition of spiritual apathy, which renders his case even less hopeful than it was before.

CHAPTER III.

WORLDLY-WISEMAN.

INTRODUCTION.—It frequently happens that when a man begins to be earnestly interested in his own spiritual welfare, he will find other persons apparently interested also. We seldom take any important step without finding many persons ready to proffer their advice, and to urge this or that line of conduct; and this will be the more observable if the interests of others are affected as well as our own. Here we are sure to have interested advisers, such as the workmen of Ephesus, who, because it was "by this craft they had their wealth," opposed that preaching of the cross of Jesus Christ which would overthrow their craft.

The world is full of claimants for man's soul. Against the righteous claims of God there are rival claims—worldly gains, worldly wisdom, worldly-mindedness, which strive to steal away man's heart from God. It is this spirit of the world that meets the Pilgrim, who has just escaped from the Slough of Despond. And while CHRISTIAN is still smarting under his recent downfall and disappointment, a man named WORLDLY-WISEMAN approaches, intent upon making him his victim, by turning him from the right way into the path of error.

This WORLDLY-WISEMAN is Self-Righteousness, that glories in the law, attributes nothing to grace, trusts to its own merit, and will not accept the merits of Christ. This Self-Righteous spirit will stand beneath Sinai, rather than look to Calvary. This legal religion would, were it possible, work its own way to heaven, and ignore the salvation that is in Christ Jesus. In the end, the folly of such a course is made manifest in the thunders, and lightnings, and threatenings of the dark and lowering Mount of Sinai. St. Paul asks such persons this solemn question—"Tell me, ye that desire to be under the law, do ye not hear the law?" Galatians 4:21. A plain answer to this question is contained in the following scene of the Pilgrim's Progress.

Walking solitarily.—PLIABLE has departed home again. HELP, having lifted the Pilgrim from the mire, has also departed, and CHRISTIAN is left alone. A Christian "walking solitarily" is sometimes a mark for temptation; while, if he would walk in company with a fellow-Christian, he would probably escape the temptation. The tempter ofttimes selects our lonely moments for his fiercest assaults. When alone, the Christian may be weak: in company with brother Christians, he may be very strong. This was evidently a weak moment to our Pilgrim—an opportunity for the assault of the evil one.

Mr. Worldly-wiseman.—The name is intended to indicate the nature of the man; as the name of his town, Carnal-policy, to illustrate his origin and associations. This is the man that walks by sight, and not by faith; talks presumptuously of human merit, ignoring the merits of Christ; clothes himself in his own righteousness, refusing the saving righteousness of Jesus. This man is of the world, carnally-minded, legally disposed; he is of those that seek to justify themselves. Their wisdom is but worldly wisdom, and this shall be outwitted at the last, and utterly turned into foolishness. They that are "wise after the flesh" are not "wise unto God."

Having some guess of him.—There were certain marks and characteristics by which CHRISTIAN was recognized by WORLDLY-WISEMAN—"by beholding his laborious going, and by observing his sighs and groans." Now these marks form the direct contrast to the spirit of the worldly-wise man. He evidences no "laborious going;" his walk is an easygoing career. If hardships should arise, and "sighs and groans" come at seasons, these troubles rise not from the depths of conscience, but only play upon the outer surface of external circumstances. He cannot, therefore, understand what it is to be deeply burdened with iniquity; nor has he ever heaved a sigh or groan from the consciousness of sin. Accordingly, by these marks of heartfelt penitence, he now discerns in our Pilgrim the man who had set forth from the City of Destruction.

Hast thou a wife and children?—This question is one of those inquiries suggested by worldly wisdom and carnal policy: earthly things first, and then (if ever) heavenly things. Farm, merchandise, wife, and children,—for one or more of these things "I pray thee have me excused;" as though the having of these could ever constitute a fitting apology for neglecting the pilgrimage of Sion.

The good and pious Archbishop Leighton was once addressed by his married sister, who was troubled about many family cares:—"*You* may serve God very well, who have no family to occupy your thoughts, nor children to call off your attention from religion." The venerable prelate thus replied, in a single text of Scripture—"And Enoch walked with God, and begat sons and daughters."*

WORLDLY-WISEMAN'S question, then, has nothing to do with this great matter. Wife and children were not given to us to keep us from God. Therefore the words of Christ—"He that loveth father or mother more than me, is not worthy of me: and he that loveth son or daughter more than me, is not worthy of me," Matthew 10:37.

Who bid thee go this way?—WORLDLY-WISEMAN by his questions evidently seeks to perplex the Pilgrim, and to dissuade him from his projected plan. He advises CHRISTIAN as soon as possible to get rid of his burden, but utterly repudiates the method suggested by the good counsel of EVANGELIST. He has no sympathy with the Pilgrim, or with the utter hopelessness of his condition, so far as human aid is concerned. Another way, he urges, must be tried; and even brings up the bemired condition of CHRISTIAN from the Slough of Despond, as a manifest proof that EVANGELIST was wrong in his directions; and then, to deter CHRISTIAN, he speaks of all sorts of difficulties and dangers; but these do not terrify the Pilgrim, for he feels the pressure of this burden to be worse to him than all possible inconveniences that may arise in the path.

How camest thou by thy burden?—This is drawing to closer quarters. The tempter already sees that there is a deep and thorough realization of the weight and weariness of the burden. He now seeks to remove—not the burden, but the *consciousness* of the burden. And first of all, he attempts to overthrow the authority of the Book which has disclosed to the Pilgrim the existence and weight of his sin. He talks at random of "distractions," and "desperate ventures," and such like; and finding that the burdened man seeks rest, and must have ease from his burden, and will not else be satisfied, WORLDLY-WISEMAN proceeds to suggest a false peace, and a rest which, after all, can give the guilty conscience no relief. He promises many things—ease, safety, friendship, and contentment.

Open this secret to me.—WORLDLY-WISEMAN has gained the Pilgrim's ear, and now he delves deeper, and gains the Pilgrim's heart. CHRISTIAN is now listening to the counsel of the ungodly. We fear for the result.

Morality, Legality, Civility.—These are the new saviors suggested by WORLDLY-WISEMAN; not far off, easily found, and prompt to ease the burden. Pretentious promises! These watchwords are "of the

---

*Genesis 5:22—And Enoch walked with God after he begat Methuselah three hundred years, and begat sons and daughters.

earth, earthy." They underrate the enormity of sin, depreciate the provisions of grace, and ignore the great salvation which is through Christ Jesus.

The village of Morality is the place where the Pharisee once dwelt (where Pharisaism still dwells), whose religion is a mere boastful profession—"I thank thee that I am not as other men are." This religion sets up claims, personal claims; and expects heaven by right of labor done and service rendered. It hides the great truth of the Christian revelation, which establishes the fact that man is *nothing*, and that Christ is *everything*; that by grace we are saved, but that "by the deeds of the law there shall no flesh be justified in his sight." Morality must ever be a characteristic of the Christian man; but it must not be his resting-place, for it is not his salvation. The spiritual life must rise higher, and live on a better principle than this! it must live "by the faith of the Son of God." It is not by making the best of our diseased condition that we can obtain life, but by seeing and knowing *the worst* of our state, and then fleeing for refuge to lay hold upon the hope—the only hope—that is set before us.

The Christian practices morality and delights in good works, not that he *may be* forgiven, but because *he is* forgiven. Morality may attend to the claims of one man upon another, and yet neglect the claims made by God; but faith works by love, and strives to be faithful to both God and man.

Legality is the character of the man who trusts in the law, and boasts of his obedience to the law. Legality doth always seek to justify itself, and for this purpose rushes into court, challenging justice, and confronting the very judge himself. Let the man who clings to the law and not to the Gospel, who professes obedience and seeks not mercy—let him stand forth before God, and see what the law saith, and what the law can do! Prepare the line, make ready the plummet; measure and gauge the outward acts, the inward motives; the thoughts, the words, and the deeds of the entire life. You have courted the law, and you shall have it. But remember the terms of the law: on the slightest deviation from perfect rectitude, or the least departure from the line laid down, your doom is sealed; for the law saith, "The soul that sinneth, it shall die."* In the soul-searching inquisition of this tribunal, who shall stand? "Judgment also will I lay to the line, and righteousness to the plummet: and the

---

*Ezekiel 18:4—Behold, all souls are mine; as the soul of the father, so also the soul of the son is mine: the soul that sinneth, it shall die.

hail shall sweep away the refuge of lies, and the waters shall overflow the hiding place," Isaiah 28:17.

WORLDLY-WISEMAN, in fact, suggests self-justification instead of self-condemnation; forgetfulness of sin, instead of earnest search for forgiveness of sin; the opiate of unconcern to lull the awakened soul to sleep; the flattering unction that will speak tenderly of the wrong doings of the man, and whisper peace, when there is no peace. And this he calls "being eased of his burden!"

Christian somewhat at a stand.—He has been giving heed to the counsel of the ungodly; he now "*standeth* in the way of sinners." He inclines to evil, and he knoweth it not.

> "I know not what came o'er me,
> Nor who the counsel gave;
> But I must hasten downward,
> All with my pilgrim-stave."*

So Christian turned.—Yes, "turned out of the way." He has despised the counsel of EVANGELIST; has followed the advice of WORLDLY-WISEMAN; and is now about to learn new experiences. Instead of the promised "ease," there is greater weight added to the burden; instead of "safety," there is impending danger from the overhanging cliff; instead of "friendship," there is the dismal loneliness of one who has ventured beyond the reach of all human aid; instead of "contentment," the Pilgrim is ill at ease, standing amid the flashes of fiery wrath, and trembling and quaking for very fear. Darkness, fire, and tempest are the companions of his path. CHRISTIAN is at the base of SINAI! He has come to the covert of the law, beneath the dark thunder-cloud; he has come, *with his burden,* to the place of condemnation. "O wretched man that I am! Who shall deliver me?"†

And did quake for fear.—The law gendereth to bondage; and the spirit of bondage is the spirit of fear. On Sinai, God is a Judge, and man a convicted criminal. On Calvary, God is a Father, and man the adopted son of his love; and "perfect love casteth out fear." CHRISTIAN now finds how true it is that "the way of transgressors is hard."

He saw Evangelist coming.—This friend and counselor has watched, as a true minister always will, the progress of the Pilgrim. He has seen him stopped in his course by WORLDLY-WISEMAN; has seen him lend his ears and heart to the voice of temptation; has seen him take the wrong direction, forsaking the path of safety; and now he

---

*Henry Wadsworth Longfellow, "Whither?"
†Romans 7:24—O wretched man that I am! who shall deliver me from the body of this death?

follows him into the very midst of his danger, once more to advise and counsel him. Thank God for his appointed Evangelists, who minister to us in holy things!

What doest thou here, Christian?—This was not the path or the destination pointed out by EVANGELIST in his former conversation; it is, indeed, the very opposite. EVANGELIST had set before him blessing, and he had chosen cursing instead. Therefore, "with a severe and dreadful countenance," he asks an account of this far-gone deviation from the right way, and the Pilgrim for a time is "speechless." He is lost in the fears and alarms of the place; lost in the sense of his own inconsistency; lost in the consciousness of his fearful mistake; lost in the shame and confusion that cover his face, when thus discovered far from the path already prescribed for him by the faithful EVANGELIST.

Lest it should fall on my head.—The law is ever threatening, always impending; it is like a drawn sword hanging overhead, suspended by a single hair. He that takes refuge beneath this overhanging wrath, will find how the law can convince of sin and punish sin, but cannot take it away; it can increase the burden, but cannot lighten it. The law is a schoolmaster, and its teaching rightly understood leads to Christ; but it is Christ alone, and not the law, that *taketh away* sin.

A better way, and shorter.—This was the tempting offer of WORLDLY-WISEMAN to the Pilgrim; and it is a temptation still in the way of thousands. But there is only *one* way, and therefore there can be no better and no shorter road. If the Pilgrims of Sion seek a Crown, they must go by the way of the Cross; if they seek a triumph, they must fight their way through the battle-field.

There came words and fire.—The voice of the law is its own confirmation. The law's demands are great and large—"*all* the heart, *all* the soul, *all* the mind, *all* the strength;"* continuance "in all things which are written in the book of the law to do them."† If this full and undivided allegiance be not rendered, the law utters its curse against the rebels. And as none can render this complete obedience and this unsinning service, the result is that "as many as are of the works of the law, are under the curse," Galatians 3:10.

Sir, is there hope?—Yes, there *is* hope. If the man will but flee

---

*Mark 12:30—And thou shalt love the Lord thy God with all thy heart, and with all thy soul, and with all thy mind, and with all thy strength: this is the first commandment.
†Galatians 3:10—For as many as are of the works of the law are under the curse: for it is written, Cursed is every one that continueth not in all things which are written in the book of the law to do them.

from the law to grace, from Sinai to the Wicket-gate, and from thence to the Cross, there is hope, good hope; hope increasing more and more at every onward step of the Pilgrim.

CHAPTER IV.

THE WICKET-GATE.

INTRODUCTION.—The Wicket-gate constitutes one of the main features of the great Dreamer's Allegory. It is an end, and it is a beginning. It concludes the Pilgrim's search for the better path, and inaugurates his entrance upon the King's highway—the way of holiness. It closes upon the weary wilderness of doubt and ignorance in which he wandered, wept, and trembled, and opens upon the road that conducts all faithful pilgrims to the Celestial City.

Some difficulty has been experienced in the interpretation of the details of this stage of the Progress. Many have expressed surprise that Bunyan should thus make his Pilgrim to enter by the Wicket-gate *with his burden,* and even to traverse a portion of the way, still cumbered with his weight of sin. And, indeed, many such difficulties will arise if we expect to find in the experience of CHRISTIAN an exact copy or type of the experience of every Pilgrim that walks that way; and therefore we may here, once for all, quote the expression of James Montgomery—"These difficulties all resolve themselves into the plain matter of fact, that the PILGRIM'S PROGRESS is the history of *one* man's experience *in full,* and the experience of many others *in part.*" Accordingly, there may be some Pilgrims who do not feel the burden of their sin to sit so heavy upon them as CHRISTIAN felt his; some who fall not so deep in Despond as CHRISTIAN did; some who arrive at the Cross of Jesus, and receive pardon and assurance at an earlier stage of the journey; some who pass through better scenes, and some through worse, than fell to the lot of the hero of the Allegory.

The phase of spiritual experience indicated here is simply this. The Pilgrim has been convinced of his sin, and the consequent peril of his state. Under this conviction he thankfully seeks the Wicket-gate, and, having found it, knocks thereat. The gate is opened to him with the hearty welcome of GOOD-WILL, and he is admitted. Now, observe, CHRISTIAN has been convinced of sin; he abhors sin, and loves it not; he earnestly desires to be rid of it. Accordingly, the love of sin is left behind; and what remains is the *weight*, or *consciousness* of sin. With repentance for the past, and with faith in Christ and his promises for the future, he enters the Narrow-way. Having entered through Christ, "the Door," he commences the Christian life by faith in Christ as the way of salvation, and is at once admitted to the privileges of the way, the first of all being the teaching of the Holy Ghost, as in the scenes of the INTERPRETER'S House. There receiving instruction for the onward path, he, by-and-by, comes by the way of the Cross to "the place of deliverance." There the burden of sin upon his conscience is removed by the *assurance* of pardon and of justifying grace.

Thus all difficulty is removed. Sin—in the love of it—cannot enter through the Wicket-gate. Sin, entertained, indulged, and unrepented of, excludes from the entering in of this door. Thus sinners, *in their sin*, enter not. But sinners, *under sin*, that is, under the consciousness of guilt, are welcomed there; as GOOD-WILL says, "We make no objections against any, notwithstanding all they have done before they come hither."

This is the "good news" of the Gospel. It is the "weary and heavy-laden" that are bid to come—under the weight and consciousness of sin; and these entering in by Jesus Christ, "the Door," and being instructed by the Spirit's teaching, are, some sooner, some later, conducted to the assurance of pardon and the fullness of forgiving love.

"Knock, and it shall be opened."—At the Wicket-gate the penitent Pilgrim knocks, and in faith knocks again, and still continues to knock, until it is opened to him by GOOD-WILL, the porter of the gate—for to such "the porter openeth" (John 10:3).

Good-will.—Most suitable name for the porter of the Wicket-gate. "Goodwill toward men" is part of the definition of the Gospel. All are invited, and all who accept the invitation are welcome.

Gave him a pull.—CHRISTIAN has escaped the dangers of Destruction, Despond, and Sinai. Yet there is danger still—yea, even to the very threshold of the gate. The whole range of its vicinity is liable to assault from Beelzebub, whose fiery darts fly thick and fast at this critical point of the pilgrimage. A burdened sinner, seeking the Savior, is the very mark that Satan hastes to assail. Hence the kind intervention of GOOD-WILL. The penitent sinner is "as a brand plucked from the burning."*

---

*Zechariah 3:2—And the LORD said unto Satan, The LORD rebuke thee, O Satan; even the LORD that hath chosen Jerusalem rebuke thee: is not this a brand plucked out of the fire?

Young pilgrims of Sion, be comforted! How oft have you felt the flying arrows of the Wicked One, just as you were about to commit yourselves to the way of righteousness. When you stood, and argued, and reasoned, and sought to make up your mind to cast in your lot with those who are journeying Sionward, how Satan has withstood you, resisted you, assailed you! He has whispered doubts about yourself—as to your fitness to come at all; doubts about God—as to his willingness to save. These are the fiery darts of the Wicked One. But as there will by-and-by be given you the shield of faith to quench these darts, so, now that you are defenseless, GOOD-WILL plucks you from the danger, and pulls you in.

This is the way.—Once within the gate, and willing to proceed, the Pilgrim is directed as to the way, and the nature of the road. It is the King's highway, that has been made by God in Christ, before the foundation of the world, and since trodden into a beaten track by patriarchs, prophets, and apostles. The turnings and twistings belong not to the road, but to the devious paths that lead out of it; and these are not narrow, but wide; not straight, but crooked.

The Pilgrim now girds up his loins for the journey. Having entered upon a godly course of life, he must first receive Christian instruction; and so, to the house of the Interpreter, where we shall see "excellent things."

CHAPTER V.

THE INTERPRETER'S HOUSE.

INTRODUCTION.—A brilliant scene here opens before us: the "Glorious Dreamer" passes in review through chambers of imagery, and in the rapt vision of his soul he sees the innermost experiences of most men, and forms those marvelous conceptions of the spiritual life, which border so nearly on the Unseen. Peculiar revelations are here vouchsafed to the man of God; and in the Interpreter's House are contained some of the boldest displays of his lofty genius, and some of the brightest imaginings of his spiritually-instructed mind.

Let us walk with CHRISTIAN and the good INTERPRETER through this gallery of illustrations, and see the great visions of the Dreamer. There is an order and arrangement here which well illustrate the PILGRIM'S PROGRESS, as a manual of Christian experience, and a guide to spiritual advancement. The burdened Pilgrim has been admitted (as we have seen in the preceding chapter) within the Wicket-gate; with faith in Christ as the only way of salvation, and yet with conscience of sin still clinging to his soul. He has now to use his opportunities, so as to be rid of his burden, and to proceed upon his way; and, as an earnest and diligent seeker after truth, the first great privilege granted to him is the privilege of instruction, admonition, and encouragement. The Pilgrim of Zion, at the outset of his journey, is ignorant and unknowing of the ways of godliness; he has enlisted in a responsible service, and must be fitted for it; he will have to do battle against enemies that shall arise to meet him in his pilgrimage, and he must therefore be disciplined for the warfare; from within and from without he will experience doubts and dangers, fightings and fears; and except a special strength be given him, he never can be a match for the antagonisms of such a journey.

Accordingly, the first stage after his admission to the highway is one of instruction at the hand of the INTERPRETER, under which name the person of the Holy Spirit is designed, in His office as Teacher. And as this scene worthily occupies the foreground of the pilgrimage, so there is also a significant progression of Divine teaching and instruction in the demonstrative lessons conveyed to the mind of the Pilgrim. For example, there is first the presence of light, by the lighting of the candle. Then direction is given as to the qualifications or marks by which the true minister of the Gospel is to be distinguished from unsound teachers. This being provided, the inward work proceeds—the subduing of indwelling sin, through the power of the Divine Word, applied to the heart by the Holy Spirit, all which is shadowed forth by the imagery of the "Dusty Parlor." There is then taught the need of Patience, which calmly abideth the issue; and the spiritual improvidence of mere Passion, which exhausts itself now, and leaves nothing for the time to come. Next is the conflict between Divine grace and the temptations of Satan, in the suggestive scene of "the Fire burning against the wall." And after these stages of experience have been thus illustrated—after the casting out of sin, and the lesson of patience in running the race, and the waging of the conflict of the inner man, the INTERPRETER discloses in a brief scene the great fight of faith in the assault of the Palace gates, and the triumphant entrance of the good soldier of Jesus Christ, after the battle of the warrior has been fought and won. Thus in one gallery of illustration the INTERPRETER presents the conflict of the true Christian from first to last, chiefly in its brighter aspect and more successful issue. He then changes the character of the imagery, and conducts the Pilgrim through the darker experiences of men—the "Dark Room;" the fair and flourishing professor enclosed within the bars of the "Iron Cage;" and, after this, the Dream of Judgment.

Thus instructed and admonished, CHRISTIAN is committed to the onward journey—his ignorance instructed, his weakness made more evident by a deeper insight into self and the circumstances and experiences of religion in the soul. Thus the Holy Spirit becomes our Teacher, and "takes of the things of God, and shows them unto us." Then, with the anxious earnestness of the expectant Pilgrim, let us now stand at the door of the Interpreter's House, and say, as CHRISTIAN did, "I was told by the man that stands at the head of this way, that if I called here, you would show me excellent things, such as would be a help to me in my journey."

The House of the Interpreter.—This whole chapter is a description of the Christian Pilgrim seeking and obtaining light, and knowledge, and instruction, from the source of all Christian teaching—the

Holy Spirit. It is the office of the Holy Spirit to reveal God's mind and will, and to explain and interpret the will and mind of God to men: "He shall receive of mine, and shall show it unto you" (John 16:14). The house of the INTERPRETER is the treasure-house of experience, where are stored up all God's provisions, and providences, and dealings with men. Out of this store-house the Spirit bestows—according to our wants, our asking, and our use of supplies already given—"grace for grace." It is the shedding of Divine light, and the pouring of Divine love, and the communication of Divine knowledge, into our hearts. God was once revealed to man in the person of his Son; he is now revealed to our hearts in the power of his Spirit.

He knocked over and over.—To this the command applies, "Ask, and ye shall receive; seek, and ye shall find; knock, and it shall be opened unto you." Here is the progression—Ask; seek; knock. Each one of these successive steps involves more energy and earnestness than that which has preceded it. The Pilgrim has "asked" the way to further instruction; he has "sought" that way, and has found it; he has "knocked" at the door of the Spirit, and it is opened to him.

"Come in."—The House of the Interpreter, as the Dwelling-place of the Spirit, is the House of Call for all nations; and all that come are welcome. "Here is a traveler"—such was the brief statement of the Pilgrim's qualification, by which he sought to find refreshment on the way "from the City of Destruction to the Mount Zion." The hungry traveler calls there for bread, and the thirsty one asks there for spiritual drink. The weary and fainting soul admitted there, is fanned by the breeze of the Spirit, and revives. The toil-worn and weather-beaten traveler there finds rest, refreshment, and repose; and, renewed in strength, he goes on his way rejoicing. Bless the Lord, O my soul, for the comforting and refreshing of the Spirit, and for these chambers of imagery that enlighten the eyes, and instruct the heart, and make known to the Pilgrim the joys and sorrows, the doubts, the dangers, and the difficulties of the way of the pilgrimage!

> "God's Interpreter art Thou,
> To the waiting ones below;
> 'Twixt them and its light mid-way
> Heralding the better day."*

He commanded to light a candle.—All is dark in the chambers of the soul, until the candle of the Lord is lighted in our hearts. It is in the spiritual as it was in the natural creation—"Darkness was upon

---

*John Greenleaf Whittier, "The Curse of the Charter-breakers."

the face of the deep. And the Spirit of God moved upon the face of the waters. And God said, Let there be light!"* Happy is the man who can say as with the Psalmist, "For thou wilt light my candle; the Lord my God will enlighten my darkness," (Psalm 18:28).

The "candle" is lighted; a "door" is opened; and that door conducts to a "private room." Here, every word is of weight, and suggests volumes of experience. The representation here is of man's soul, as a dark place, its doors and windows closed. It is the secret chamber, the private room, where the Spirit now holds intercourse with man; but first the door must be opened, and the darkness illumined by the bright shining of the candle. "The entrance of thy words giveth light," (Psalm 119:130).

The Picture.—The first revelation of the Spirit to the burdened Pilgrim is as to the true character of a servant of God, to minister to him in the things of God. The Spirit fits and prepares his servants, and honors the faithful labor of those who go forth as his disciples, to be the teachers of his truth.

Space would fail us to set forth these glorious dreams in the fullness of their meaning. They need meditation and contemplation, the bringing of the mind's eye to bear upon the bold outline, and the power of Christian experience to fill up the finer tints that go to make up the perfection of each picture. Here is the minister of Christ as he ought to be: "Eyes lifted up to heaven"—heavenly-minded, looking towards that place whither he would lead the flock. From earth to heaven his office tends, and he, with purpose fixed, earnest and intent on yonder home—

> "Allures to brighter worlds, and leads the way."†

"The best of books in his hand"—the BIBLE, from whence he himself derives the truth, and knows the mind of God; and therefore, from it alone can he impart Divine knowledge to the people. "The law of truth upon its lips"—no uncertain sound, or doubtful utterance of the oracle; seeing that he is a guide, an adviser, a shepherd, nought else but Truth upon his lips can suffice for the safe leading of the sheep. "The world behind his back"—not the foreground, but the background of the picture, is the world. How disinterested, how unworldly, how self-denying, should the Gospel minister be, with earth kept ever

---

*Genesis 1:2–3—And the earth was without form, and void; and darkness was upon the face of the deep. And the Spirit of God moved upon the face of the waters. And God said, Let there be light: and there was light.
†Thomas Wentworth Higginson, "Allures to Brighter Worlds and Leads the Way."

back, and heaven kept full in view. "It pleaded with men"—in all the earnestness of one who doth "beseech men," so blind, and deaf, and dead to their own true interests, that they may be reconciled unto God. With an essential truth, a message for life or death, and eternity depending on the issue, how can the servant of God do aught else than "plead" with men? "A crown of gold over his head"—the reward of the righteous; and all the more bejeweled because of the many conquests he hath won, and souls that have been saved, which shall be his joy and crown of rejoicing in that day.

This is a representation that is to linger in CHRISTIAN'S mind and memory all through the pilgrimage, seeing that many false teachers, as wolves in sheep's clothing, would present themselves at various times and seasons, to the great peril of all who hear them.

The Dusty Parlor.—This symbol is, no doubt, designed to strengthen the impression already made upon the Pilgrim's mind by the scene at Sinai. The dust of the "Dusty Parlor" is indwelling sin. The besom of the law awakes the slumbering dust, revives its power, and causes it to be sensibly felt. Disturbed from its settled state, and discovered to our eyes, the dust of sin rises as a cloud of witness, witnessing against us. The law can disturb sin and arouse it, but the law cannot take it away. Then comes the Gospel, with the sprinkled waters of Christ's atoning love, which bind sin and repress it. The power of the law and the Gospel respectively, with regard to sin, receives here one of the most telling illustrations that uninspired man has ever written. This scene, indeed, well describes those two scriptures—"I had not known sin, but by the law," (Romans 7:7); and, "Behold the Lamb of God, which *taketh away* the sin of the world," (John 1:29).

Passion and Patience.—PASSION is as a desolating army that ravages the land, and eats from hand to mouth the growing harvests, as yet unripe; leaving no seed for the sower of the coming seed-time. PATIENCE plants the seed now, in hope of the future harvest; and waits for the timely season to render back its thirty-fold, its sixty-fold, or its hundred-fold. PATIENCE walks by faith, while PASSION walks by sight. PASSION, like the Prodigal, hath his portion now, and spends it here; whereas PATIENCE hath his portion hereafter, and enjoys it throughout eternity; or, as Bunyan puts it, "He that has his portion last, must have it lastingly."

A Fire burning against the Wall.—This is an eloquent symbol of the living Christian, whose spiritual life is fed from secret sources, while the enemy constantly seeks to destroy its vitality. The life of the man of God is ofttimes likened to a burning fire. At first it is but a spark kindled in the breast, and this is fanned by the breath of the Spirit, and fed with the fuel of Divine love—the oil of grace, directly supplied by the hand of God. This is its heavenly food, and by this it lives. But, saith St. Paul, "I see another law in my members, warring against the law of my mind." So, the dreamer beholds the fire struggling against fearful odds; for one stood beside it, and did continually pour water upon it to quench it. But the fire did not die, was not extinguished, but rather burned "higher and hotter."

In this is set forth the antagonism of Satan to man's soul; as also the overcoming power of sustaining grace, "the secret of the Lord, which is with them that fear him." Satan stands at our right hand, and would utterly quench the inner life, were it not that Christ is with us, pouring the oil of grace upon the soul. And this is our security, that "many waters cannot quench" the flame of Divine love when it is truly kindled in the heart. Even the "smoking flax" shall not be quenched; for Jesus stands, unseen, but truly felt, and in secret he supplies the grace Divine; and when the quenching waters fall in torrents, and the flame burns its weakest, then comes the reassuring word, "My grace is sufficient for thee;" and God doth strengthen the things that remain, that are ready to die. The oil of grace feeds the flame. The might of Jesus is greater than all the power of Satan.

The Ink-horn and the Book.—This is a battle-scene, and it truly describes the entrance-door to heaven, and the striving and the life-long conflict by which an entrance is effected. It is designed to show to the Pilgrim, what we have already endeavored to point out in the context of the "Wicket-gate," that there is still a great warfare to be waged, a strife to be maintained; and that through the clash of arms and the battle of the warrior, the Christian soldier must pass to the final victory and triumph. CHRISTIAN on viewing this scene, smiled, and thought he saw the meaning of it. Yes, he there saw his own future conflict, and (if he be but steadfast) the type and earnest of his final victory.

The Dark Room and Iron Cage.—This man was "very sad," with downcast eyes, his hands folded in the terribleness of despair, and his heart breaking, and well-nigh broken, by the heavy woe that had fallen upon it. This man was once "profession;" he is now "despair;" he sees no light, entertains no hope, and knows no liberty. Whether such a state as this is "of God," or no, we do not say; but it appears that Bunyan interweaves certain facts of his own experience in this portion of the Allegory. He had known some of his friends to have been thus reduced to desperation, and to have lost all confidence in God. Any way, it is an awful admonition, this particular scene of the Interpreter's House.

The danger of mere profession, without corresponding fruit, is set forth in the miracle of our blessed Lord, which he wrought upon the fruitless fig-tree, (Mark 11:12–14, 19–22). This was a pretentious tree, and by its profusion of leaves it attracted the notice of the Savior, who came seeking fruit, but found "nothing but leaves." That fig-tree is the emblem of a dead faith, a profitless profession of religion; and, lo, by the way-side it is blighted, and blasted, and withered away! Mere professors shall, at the last, be uprooted from the soil, which has spent its sap and strength for naught in feeding them; they shall be blighted even in the full foliage of their profession; and in their fall they shall make all men see the visitation of God's hand, and the power of his Word.

The Dream of Judgment.—This is the closing scene of the Interpreter's House, as its great subject—the Judgment—will be the closing scene of the world's great history. In that dream, the dreamer has seen and heard all the terrible accompaniments and associations of the final Judgment. The eye of the Judge was fixed upon him, as though he stood alone for judgment; and his sins rose up and gathered round him, as witnesses against his soul. The dreamer had awakened in the midst of these terrors, and therefore "he shook and trembled."

This is a true description of the final Judgment; but it is the Judgment of sinners. This is pre-eminently the dream of an unconverted man, conscious of his sin, but as yet unable to look to the Savior of sinners; it is but the transcript of the waking thoughts, and fears, and consciences of the ungodly.

But the Judgment has no such terrors to them that are in Jesus, That great day shall be a day of joy and blessedness to all them that wait for the promised advent of the Lord, "looking for that blessed hope, and the glorious appearing of the great God and our Savior Jesus Christ," Titus 2:13.

Hast thou considered all these things?—This is not mere idle sight-seeing; these scenes are the deep experiences of men—what they feel, what they fear, what they hope, and what they do. "Hast *thou* considered them?" CHRISTIAN has seen and pondered them. He is undergoing a process of instruction, and thus partaking of the privileges of the way on which he has entered. So far he is—as many are—with more or less consciousness of sin, repairing to the teaching of the INTERPRETER, the Holy Spirit, who will yet lead the Pilgrim onward on the road; beyond the chequered scenes of his pilgrimage, and conduct him by the way of the Cross to the everlasting Crown.

> "No fears disturb, no foes molest,
> Nor death, nor sin, nor care,
> In Thy fair house of endless rest,
> O Great Interpreter!"

CHAPTER VI.

THE CROSS AND THE CONTRAST.

INTRODUCTION.—Since the Pilgrim's entrance on the Narrow-way, through the appointed "door," the Wicket-gate, he has not only been made a partaker of great and precious privileges, in the direct teaching of the INTERPRETER, but he has also corresponded well with those privileges; and, deeply impressed with the lessons he has learned, he now proceeds along a safe and well-guarded portion of the way—safe, because it was enclosed on either side, and strongly fenced with walls, which were called "Salvation." Along the "Way of Salvation" the burdened Pilgrim, with somewhat of haste, and with somewhat of difficulty too, urges his upward journey. Here he comes in full view of the Cross, and near the Cross, in the hollow, is a Sepulcher. In sight of the Cross he receives the long wished for, the long prayed for deliverance; the thongs and bands that bound his burden to his back are burst asunder, and the burden falls off, and rolls down, and at last disappears for ever through the open mouth of the Sepulcher. All is now rest and peace, life, light, and liberty, mingled with wonder and astonishment, and tempered with the tears of joy.

The desired ease from his burden is straightway followed by further evidences of his deliverance. The salutation in common of the "Three Shining Ones," and then the individual gift or message of each: one gives Pardon; another clothes with Change of raiment; while the third bestows the assurance of the Mark, the credential of the Roll, and the impress of the Seal.

> "'Peace be to thee'—all declaring;
>   One forgives him all his sin;
> One, a change of raiment bearing,
>   Clothes without, and clothes within.
>
> Then the third, his finger tracing,
>   Prints a mark upon his brow;
> And a roll his hand embracing,
>   With a signet sealed below."

In the character and circumstances of the personages subsequently introduced some profitable contrasts are suggested. This chapter contains some remarkable delineations of characters to be met with on the pilgrimage, such as SIMPLE, SLOTH, and PRESUMPTION; and the two men who came leaping over the wall, FORMALIST and HYPOCRISY. These professors of the Christian faith, having the form of godliness but not the power, will be found to have entered, not by the appointed door, but by some one or other of the "many ways that butt down" upon the beaten track.

Fenced on either side.—The allusion here is to the figurative language of the prophet—"Salvation will God appoint for walls and bulwarks," Isaiah 26:1; and again, "And thou shalt call thy walls Salvation, and thy gates Praise," Isaiah 60:18. And although the direct application of these texts is to the final blessedness of the saints, yet the allusion is well adapted in a secondary sense to those who, like our Pilgrim, instructed and edified by the Holy Spirit's comfort, counsel, and encouragement, are drawing near to the foot of the Cross of Jesus.

A place somewhat ascending.—The Cross is erected on the height of an upward slope, even higher than the upward path. This is to indicate the ascent of Calvary, the Mount of Sacrifice; and also to suggest, not so much the toil of the burdened sinner to attain to it, as the toil of the burdened Savior, who bare not only our sin, but the Cross besides, up that "ascending place," and there paid the full ransom for man's iniquity in the price of his own most precious blood.

A Cross.—Blessed view! and yet, more blessed still,

> "The Man that there was put to shame for me!"

The Cross here means the Crucified One. It is the emblem of all that scorn and ignominy, of all that pain and agony, borne by Him who "took our sins, and bare them in his own body on the tree." The benefit procured by the death upon the Cross was the object of the Pilgrim's striving; the central point to which his hopes converged; the source of all the blessed experiences of his after pilgrimage. There was "the blood of sprinkling;" there the atoning Lamb; there the substitute for the sinner; and there the sacrifice for sin. Christ and the Cross! Here is the Altar, and the Victim, and the Priest; and in the Crucified One the scheme of redemption is accomplished—"IT IS FINISHED!"

A Sepulcher.—Well is the Sepulcher placed hard by the Cross. In the crucified Jesus the debt is cancelled, and the bond is nailed to the accursed tree. "He took it out of the way, *nailing it to his cross,*" Colossians 2:14.

His burden loosed, and fell.—Sin is described not only as a burden, but as a burden *bound* upon the conscience of the Pilgrim—adhering, clinging, to the sinner, who is "tied and bound with the chain of sin." These bands are now unloosed in view of the Cross; and the burden falls from off his back.

And I saw it no more.—The Bible represents forgiven sin as being "blotted out;" "no more remembered;" "sought for, but not found;" "cast into the depths of the sea." It sleeps its everlasting sleep, to rise no more.

Then was Christian glad.—The Wicket-gate. There was the threshold of his journey, but here is the threshold of his joy. There he became a Christian in prospect—his faith weak and trembling; here he becomes a Christian in deed and in truth—his faith assured and confident.

Behold, Three Shining Ones.—This is one of the most picturesque of the touches of Bunyan's pencil. These are the evidences of the deliverance from the burden and accompaniments of sin. Yea, they are more: these "Three Shining Ones" are plainly intended to represent no less a visitation than that of Unity in Trinity and Trinity in Unity. This will further appear by considering the particulars of their visit.

They all saluted the Pilgrim with one common salutation—"Peace be to thee." Here the Three are One.

Then each of the glorious Three has a personal and peculiar office to fulfill, and some special gift to bestow.

The First says—"Thy sins be forgiven thee." This is God the Father, to whom belongs pardon and forgiveness.

The Second "stripped him of his rags, and clothed him with change of raiment." This is Jesus Christ—God the Son. He takes away the rags of our own righteousness, and clothes us with the new robe of his own righteousness—the righteousness from heaven. It is an exchange—not the putting of Christ's righteousness *over* our filthy rags, but the gift of Christ's righteousness *instead of* our filthy rags.

The Third "set a mark upon his forehead, and gave him a roll with a seal upon it." This is evidently the Holy Spirit, who "beareth witness with our spirit, that we are the children of God," Romans 8:16. He imprints the Mark of ownership, the token that we are of

God. He gives the roll of the parchment—the law written on our hearts—upon which the Pilgrim is to look, and out of which he is to read, and thence to take comfort, admonition, and instruction, and to present it by-and-by at the gate of the Celestial City. The seal is "the seal of the Spirit," to certify the credential, and authenticate its message.

Thus all the Three Persons of the Triune God have a work to do for man, and each his own respective office to fulfill, in the *Pardon*, the *Justification*, and the *Sanctification* of the sinner. And this great doctrine and fact is thus luminously embodied in the scene at the Cross, and in the appearance of the "Three Shining Ones."

Three men fast asleep.—As though to exhibit by contrast the greatness of the gift he has received, and the responsibility arising therefrom, CHRISTIAN is permitted, in passing, to witness the folly, indolence, and pride of certain carnal men, who count themselves safe and exempt from danger, and who, in their fancied security, have all fallen "fast asleep."

They are "out of the way," though but "a little;" they are "asleep;" and they are, moreover, bound in "fetters;" and, worst of all, the Roaring Lion is out upon the way. CHRISTIAN strives to awake these sleepers, and to warn them of their danger. Such, indeed, is the blessed toil of those who have felt in their own experience the power of pardoning grace, and the peace of pardoned sin; they go forth to win others to their great Savior's cause.

"I see no danger."—There are thousands who are only "a little" out of the way, who are in the very midst of deadly peril, and can yet "see no danger," notwithstanding.

"A little more sleep."—The deep sleep of sloth and slumber has proved fatal to many on the border-land of the pilgrimage. They have oft-times slept too long, and sometimes have overslept their day of grace, and been waked too late "to wrestle with the dread of death."

"Every vat," etc.—PRESUMPTION is the scorner among these three. He rejects the proffered counsel, on the ground of his own merit, and is ready to hold himself responsible for the consequences.

Tumbling over the wall.—This is another of the contrasts that quickly follow upon the scene at the Cross—two men entering the "Narrow way" by unlawful means. They leap over the wall on the "left hand"—the place of the wicked in the judgment; thereby indicating not only the unlawful violence of their act, but also the evil character of the men.

Formalist—Hypocrisy.—These are their names, and their nature agreeth thereto. The former is the type of those who, by an external show of religion, deceive themselves; while the latter represents those who, under guise of their hypocrisy, seek to deceive others. The formalist, through his outward attention to mere ritual observances, blinds his own eyes to his own inward state, and oft-times takes for granted that where the gilded setting is, there the precious jewel must be—a grand mistake, and a strong delusion! The hypocrite, knowing that all is wrong within, bedecks himself without with pretence and falsehood, and thus blinds the eyes of others.

"If we are in, we are in."—This is a plausible speech indeed! Yet out of this their boasted possession of the way arises the bold contrast between themselves and the Pilgrim. He has entered by the appointed "door;" they have entered as thieves and robbers, climbing up some other way. He walks by his Master's rule; they by their own fancies. They are false at the start, and cannot be true at the end. Other grand distinctions in costume and character are enumerated by the Pilgrim.

CHAPTER VII.

THE HILL DIFFICULTY.

INTRODUCTION.—The preceding chapter has presented characters in contrast. The Pilgrim of Sion meets with strange comrades in the way. We have already considered his conversation with the two men who came leaping over the wall—FORMALIST and HYPOCRISY. These men flippantly talked of their fancied security, and could see no difference between their own state and that of CHRISTIAN'S. The Pilgrim recounts many marks and tokens enjoyed by him, and not possessed by them. But as these marks and tokens, to be appreciated, must be "spiritually discerned," and as these two men have no gift of spiritual discernment, they cannot see that there is so great a difference between their lot and his.

And, perhaps, by the outward eye, and from external appearance, these marks and tokens of the Divine favor are not observable. Indeed, it oft-times sorely tried the mind of the Psalmist, thus beholding the ungodly prospering in the way. He at last, however, found the solution of the difficulty—"Until I went into the sanctuary of God; then understood I *their end,*" Psalm 73:17. Yes, it is the "end" of these men that makes the vast distinction; and this perspective view of the case of FORMALIST and HYPOCRISY seems to have been in the mind of CHRISTIAN when he said to them—"You came in by yourselves without his direction, and shall go out by yourselves without his mercy."

Accordingly, the separation soon takes place. By-and-by the path divides in three. The "Narrow way" is *up* the hill, straight before the Pilgrims. This steep ascent is called Difficulty, and CHRISTIAN addresses himself to climb the hill. On either side of the ascending path there lay a level road; one to the left hand, and another to the right. One was called Danger, and the other was Destruction. By these roads the two Pilgrims wended their way, each to the ruin of his soul. CHRISTIAN proceeded up the hill; and here we must pause and consider carefully the experience obtained at this stage of his journey—the Pleasant Arbor; his untimely sleep; the dark shades of evening fast descending; and how, amid the alarms and terrors of the way, "he felt in his bosom for his roll . . . he felt, and found it not."

> " 'Tis gone! and the darkness more gloomy than ever,
> Like sadness that always accompanies loss,
> Compels him to seek, if he yet may recover,
> The Roll of the Parchment he found at the Cross."

The hill Difficulty.—Who that has been at the foot of the Cross has not also had to meet the difficulties of the way? These are tests, provided for "the trial of our faith." The way is straight and narrow, but it is not always level.

At the bottom was a spring.—Not without some special provision is the Pilgrim committed to this special difficulty. The spring of water is placed at the foot of the hill for the refreshment of pilgrims before they begin the ascent. The waters of life refresh the soul, renew the strength, and enable us more bravely to meet the difficulties of the way. "All my springs are in thee," Psalm 87:7.

Two other ways.—But where are FORMALIST and HYPOCRISY? "If we are in, we are in," said they, in the day of their boastful profession. But the hill Difficulty has stopped them; and, unequal to its demands upon their strength, they betake themselves right and left, to the "two other ways," that *promised* to obviate the difficulty of the ascent, and to conduct to the same destination by-and-by. The result is well described in the names of these two paths—Danger and Destruction.

Running, going, clambering.—Here is the Christian man brought face to face with some hard lot, some unlooked-for test and trial of his faith. He cheerfully meets the difficulty, and with prayerful energy and energetic supplication he still climbs the steep ascent of Difficulty—"running, going, clambering."

A pleasant arbor.—There are times of refreshing that come from the presence of the Lord. The shade of this cool retreat, and the refreshment of this half-way house, enable the Pilgrim to enjoy for a time some of the privileges he had received at the Cross. He reads in his roll, and is comforted. But ere long the wearied traveler nods to sleep, and by-and-by he has out-slept many precious hours of the day, and night is drawing on. He is awakened by a voice of admonition, and again starts upon his journey.

Timorous and Mistrust.—These two men, returning from the onward journey, with stories of lions and other dangers, represent the fightings without and the fears within which agitate the soul during seasons of unfaithfulness or relapse. These men had no certain knowledge of the dangers that alarmed them. They did not tarry fairly to inquire what were the dangers, and how they might be overcome, but at the first influence of fear they beat a hasty retreat, and departed.

I will yet go forward.—This is the determination of CHRISTIAN'S better nature. His faith enables him to weigh the certainties against the probabilities of the case. To go back is certain death; to go forward is only *fear* of death. To return to Destruction is to perish; to march on to the Celestial City is life, and safety, and salvation. Here is the Christian man triumphing over doubts and difficulties; for while some of his companions on the way turn aside, and others linger behind, he pursues his onward course.

He felt for his roll.—Though he has subdued his fears and misgivings, yet, after this conflict with opposing doubts, he feels the need of comfort, and accordingly betakes himself to the roll of the parchment. But he finds it not as at other times. He has lost it! Yes, he has lost the roll of his acceptance—the passport of his journey, the guide and counselor of his pilgrimage, his credential at the gate of bliss. This is a great loss.

But straightway he bethinks himself of his sleep in the arbor on the hill, and determines to retrace his footsteps. It is well when the conscience can thus recall the memory of the false step, and recognize the beginning of error, and address itself to the restoration of the loss sustained thereby.

CHRISTIAN, now retracing his steps, seeks to recover the lost credential. This is always weary work, filled with repinings and self-reproaches. Hence the feeling of the Pilgrim's mind; he sighed, and wept, and did chide himself. This retreating journey is meant to indicate the painful ordeal and the anxious interval between conviction of a specific sin and the return of confidence by the restoration of the sinner. This disquietude of spiritual experience is felt in smaller as in larger deviations, according as the conscience is tender, sensitive, and true. In the "Life of Hedley Vicars," we are told what was the effect upon that young Christian's mind of one occasion of neglect of private devotion. "My soul was the worse for it," he said, "for nearly three weeks afterwards."

He spied his roll.—These darksome days, no doubt, ofttimes overcast the pilgrimage; but earnest faith will strive to look through them; and by diligence, and prayer, and assisting grace, the Pilgrim will work out of them, and regain his lost assurance and confidence in God. CHRISTIAN has now recovered the loss of the roll; he once again has peace with God.

The sun went down.—Although sin may be forgiven, and confidence restored, there will yet be felt for a time the evil consequences of our offending. In this case, many valuable hours of the work-day had been lost in sleep, and still further loss had been sustained in striving to recover the missing roll. The consequence is that eventide and nightfall descend on the Pilgrim ere he has accomplished that day's journey; and with the darkness all the associations of darkness gather round him—the fears and fancies, the terrors and alarms of the night season. The story of the lions, too, seems to him to be more likely to be true; and his disquietude is therefore all the more augmented.

A very stately palace.—God is with the Pilgrim, and His providence conducts him; so that, in the midst of his sorrows and bewailings, he is guided to a place of light, and comfort, and refreshment—the Palace Beautiful—one of those resting-places on the way, which are designed to impart fresh spiritual light and new spiritual strength, ere the Pilgrim betakes himself to the greater perils and more grave responsibilities of the onward journey.

CHAPTER VIII.

THE PALACE BEAUTIFUL.

INTRODUCTION.—Hitherto the Pilgrim has trod a solitary path; he has been alone; and, with the exception of EVANGELIST'S timely counsels, he has had no brotherly communion or companionship with Christian men. His brother pilgrims on the road have been, till now, intruders upon the King's highway, and therefore their progress has soon ended, and their companionship has been as brief as it was unprofitable.

It is now time to introduce the Pilgrim to the Communion of Saints, and to the privilege of Christian intercourse. This is an essential part of every pilgrim's progress to the Better Land. The "narrow way" is not so very strait but that we may have companions there, and travel in a goodly company towards Zion. CHRISTIAN has lacked this spiritual intercourse, and now he must have it; and, accordingly, when he lacks it most, he receives it most plentifully. This stage of the Christian journey brings us to a home, where Christian virtues dwell, and all the things that are lovely and of good report, the things that accompany salvation; a household dedicated to thy cause, Thou Savior of the lost!—

> "Where every heart goes forth to meet thee,
> Where every ear attends thy word;
> Where every lip with blessing greets thee,
> Where all are waiting on their Lord!"*

In the Palace Beautiful our Pilgrim finds comfort, refreshment, and renewed strength, after the loneliness and desolation of that memorable day, and that eventful eventide. All his loss of peace, and loss of confidence, and loss of time is now compensated by the unspeakable gain of this godly communion and Christian fellowship, in which he abides from day to day, and through which he is enabled, in Christian conversation, to review the past, thereby impressing the thoughts and scenes of the pilgrimage more and

---

*Karl Johann Philipp Spitta, "O Happy House."

more upon his mind and conscience. His external circumstances, and the concerns of his inward state, form profitable topics of conversation with those who fear the Lord. CHRISTIAN is thereby refreshed in his mind; he is instructed more deeply in the things of God, and in the wondrous histories of his servants. He is, moreover, *armed* for his future conflicts, and is shown some effects of the might and prowess of the brave warriors and good soldiers of the Cross who have passed that way before him. He is allowed to see afar off the Delectable Mountains, and Emmanuel's Land; and to that prospect is added this promise—"When thou comest there, from thence thou mayest see to the gates of the Celestial City."

He espied two lions.—These were probably the lions that MISTRUST and TIMOROUS saw, and by the sight of which they were turned back again. These lions were placed in a narrow path, so that there appeared but little way of escape for those that would pass by that way.

Many apparent spiritual dangers seem formidable until they are more closely examined by the eye of faith and with confidence in God. Ignorance ofttimes exaggerates threatening danger, as it sees not and knows not the restraining power of Divine grace. MISTRUST and TIMOROUS could not tell whether the lions were "sleeping" or "waking;" the very sight of the lions in the distance alarmed them. CHRISTIAN'S ignorance, too, had well nigh driven him back; for "the lions were chained, but *he saw not* the chains." It was the kind and timely voice of the porter, WATCHFUL, that dispelled his fears by dispelling his ignorance, informing him that these lions were for the probation of faith, and would be harmless if he would only walk in the middle of the path.

How greatly do these messages of God's ambassadors strengthen the pilgrims of Sion and embolden them in the midst of danger! Here were rampant, roaring lions; not asleep, but awake, in a narrow passage, and very near; but they were "chained." This announcement makes all the difference. MISTRUST and TIMOROUS might also have heard the good Porter's news, only they came not near enough, but fled at the first view of the seeming danger. Suspicion is the child of little knowledge; therefore let it know more, and see more thoroughly. Knowledge looks with open face, and therefore sees all things plainly.

There are some who think they see in this story of "the lions" a political allusion to the civil penalties and disabilities of the period.

This is not at all improbable, though the expression is so worded as to convey a purely spiritual meaning to the reader. This, indeed, is one of the excellences of the PILGRIM'S PROGRESS, that it is written for all time; and even long after its local and political allusions have been lost sight of, its deep spiritual meaning remains, for the admonition and encouragement of pilgrims.

What house is this?—As yet he knows not what provision of grace is here stored up for him. He has realized his loss; has suffered by delay; has been alarmed by the darkness and other dangers; and now a light suddenly appears, and a stately mansion by the wayside. This is the Palace Beautiful, with its fair inhabitants, and its blessed companionships, and its heavenly communion, and its rich store of provision for the onward scenes and stages of the Pilgrimage—another house of call for the wayfaring pilgrims of Sion. It is of the Lord's own building; it is the Master's own merciful appointment—"for the relief and security of pilgrims." There they are housed in the time of peril; there "shut in" till greater strength is given for greater need; and forth from the fellowship of the saints they proceed upon their way, stronger, wiser, better men.

My name was Graceless.—From the outset of the pilgrimage the Pilgrim has been called by the name of CHRISTIAN. But this was not always his name. This is his "new name." And before this was given him, he was called GRACELESS. This was the name by which he was called in the City of Destruction, until God opened his eyes to behold his state in sin, and gave him grace to flee from the wrath to come. He was by nature *without grace*, and therefore GRACELESS; but now he is *with Christ*, and therefore is he called by the name of CHRISTIAN.

The sun is set.—Ah, here again is the remembrance of his sin—that sleep which he slept in the arbor on the hill. That slumber, and the loss of his evidence, kept him back from the communion of saints and from the refreshment of Christian intercourse. Alas, how these sins intercept the path, and hinder the journey! By the time that sleep is slept out, and the roll lost, and the loss discovered, and the missing evidence regained, and the hill climbed again, the day has been far spent, and "the sun has set."

Weary and benighted.—It is very plain that this palace was designed as a refuge for the wayfarer, and that its asylum would be most acceptable to those pilgrims who are most exposed to the sorrows and hardships of the way. Christian communion is at all times useful, but particularly so when we meet with spiritual losses, and consequently experience more or less of spiritual depression. In days of weariness, and nights clouded with gloom, how reassuring is the pressure of a friendly hand, the encouragement of a familiar voice, the company of a faithful friend!

For relief and security of pilgrims.—This was the twofold use of the Palace Beautiful—"relief" from the toil and travail of the road, and "security" from danger, seen and unseen, present and to come.

The principal members of this household of faith are called DISCRETION, PRUDENCE, PIETY, and CHARITY. By these names are indicated the heavenly virtues and the graces of the Spirit: DISCRETION appertaining to the intellect and judgment; PRUDENCE affecting the interests of the life now present and also of that which is to come; PIETY regulating the devotions of the soul and spirit; and CHARITY discharging all the duties of love to God and to our fellow-men. Some one has pithily remarked, in reference to this scene and stage of the Pilgrim's experience—"How 'beautiful' must that Church be where WATCHFUL is the porter; where DISCRETION governs; where PRUDENCE takes the oversight; where PIETY conducts the worship; and where CHARITY endears the members one to another!"

The introduction of the Pilgrim to the palace devolves upon DISCRETION, who also conducts the preliminary conversation. She ascertains the past history of CHRISTIAN—whence he has come, and whither he is going. He is also straitly questioned as to how he entered the way; for none can be made partakers of the blessedness of that fair house and of its goodly company, but they who have entered by the Wicket-gate. Last of all, she inquires his name. Names are no passport in spiritual things; it is the inward man, and not the outward name, that ensures admittance to the true fellowship of the saints and of the household of God. Therefore, not the first, but the last of the questions, is that concerning the Pilgrim's name.

In the conversations that ensue, PIETY is the first to speak. She inquires into the inward motives that prompted the Pilgrim to this pilgrimage. CHRISTIAN'S answer to this inquiry opens up afresh the memory of his flight from the City of Destruction. He tells of the "dreadful sound" by which he was "driven out" of his native land. Wrath from without, conviction from within, and both these working upon conscience—deep calling unto deep—created that "dreadful sound," so that the man was "driven" to flight. The further questions proposed by PIETY reproduce the narrative of the preceding scenes of the pilgrimage, including the Wicket-gate, the illustrations of the Interpreter's House, the sight of One who did hang bleeding upon a tree, the tokens and credentials given him at the Cross, and the unworthy companions that met him on the way. Then the Pilgrim reports progress, and explains his past experiences.

PRUDENCE next engages the Pilgrim in conversation. She enters not so much into the motives and feelings of the past, as into his thoughts and feelings for the present—those inward phases of the soul's reflection, when, having forsaken the old things, a new life is to be lived, on new and better principles. It is important we should ourselves inquire whether any vain regrets intertwine themselves with our present obedience; whether an earnest strife is waged against the carnal thoughts that rise within us; and whether that strife is crowned with victory, so that carnal things are "vanquished," and die within us.

The "golden hours" of the Pilgrim's triumphs over carnal things, and holy contemplation of heavenly things, are seasons much to be desired—those blessed seasons of the soul's health and well-being, when the Cross is held full in view, and the glory of the Robe of Righteousness is seen, and the comforts of the Roll refresh the spirit, and all the blissful thoughts and prospects of final blessedness kindle the fire of a holy fervor and enthusiasm in the man of God. Ay, these are the thoughts that lift us heavenward—the hope of meeting with the Living Lord, and of finding full exemption from the influence of sin, and the endless enjoyment of immortality; and all these feelings quickened by the love we bear to Jesus, who hath first loved us, and hath redeemed us from sin and death.

CHARITY continues the communion and fellowship of heart with heart. She inquires about his home and family, and how it is they have not joined him in his pilgrimage, and whether blame attaches to him for any neglect on his part of their spiritual interests. To all these inquiries CHRISTIAN answers truthfully and well. His wife would not resign the world and the pleasures of the world; and his children would not surrender the pleasures of youth; and thus did the spell of worldliness bind them to carnal things. CHRISTIAN witnesses a good confession before these damsels of the palace, and is commended for his faithful efforts to win his family to Christ— "Thou hast delivered thy soul from their blood!"

This allusion to the number of his children answers to the number of Bunyan's family, at the time of his writing the PROGRESS. He had a wife, two sons, and two daughters. Mr. Offor informs us, in a note to his edition, that "this conversation was first published in the second edition, 1678." At that time, however, his wife and children were fellow-pilgrims with their father. Mr. Offor further observes, that Bunyan's "eldest, son was a preacher eleven years before the second part of the PILGRIM was published."

Now I saw in my dream.—The dream continues; their sweet communion has not yet ended. From words of conversation, the sisters of the household conduct their guest to "a feast of fat things" for his refreshment. Whether Bunyan means by this the ordinary domestic entertainment of Christian fellowship, or the more spiritual feast—the Supper of the Lord, we do not here decide. We think he has wisely and judiciously left it open to either interpretation, or both. But this much, at all events, is evident, that "all their talk at the table was about the Lord of the Hill." Well is it for those families and those communions whose talk is of Jesus when they meet together for bodily or for spiritual refreshment: "Whether therefore ye eat, or drink, or whatsoever ye do, do all to the glory of God." (1 Corinthians 10:31.)

Christian communion on the subject of the Savior tends to elicit some precious truths respecting his nature, his work, and the provision he hath made for the wayfaring pilgrims of Sion. This conversation, for instance, altogether tends to magnify the exceeding great *love* of Jesus, as manifested in all that he hath done and suffered for sinners. His character as the Great Captain of our salvation is here enlarged upon—the battles he hath fought, and the conquests he hath won in the interests of fallen and sinful man; and how he hath slain the great enemy of souls. And in all these glorious deeds, the one great motive was love—the love of God, the love of Jesus; that love of country, yea, even of rebellious citizens, which lifts the character of Christ far beyond that of the noblest and most self-denying patriot that ever suffered for his country's cause. In this conversation those Divine characteristics of Jesus are discussed, which illustrate his gracious condescension and love: how he descended from his royal throne—this was his self-resignation; how he condescended to the low level of our lot—this was his self-abasement; how he trod the patient path of human suffering—this was his self-denial; and how he climbed the mount of Calvary—this was his self-sacrifice. And having paid the purchase of redemption, he would not have his death to be a profitless or barren sacrifice; but, through it, would conduct many sons to glory; lifting up the beggar from the dunghill, and making the children of Sion to be princes in all lands.

Such was the communion of these confiding and trusting souls, conveying large stores of strength and spiritual consolation into the Pilgrim's heart.

> "Who can tell the joy, the bliss,
> Of communion such as this!
> 'These have been,' let others say,
> 'At the gates of heaven today.'"*

The Christian, while sojourning at this blissful portion of his journey heavenward, discovers, by searching his own heart, by converse with godly companions, and by a frequent inspection of the Roll which EVANGELIST gave him, that God is wise in his teachings and gracious in his dealings: appearing by his dispensations to say to the inexperienced—"I have many things to say unto you, but ye cannot bear them now; but what ye know not now, ye shall know hereafter;" and therefore that God in tenderness imparts wisdom to the Christian according to his ability to receive it, and appoints conflicts also in proportion to his strength to resist them. In addition to this lesson of heavenly wisdom, CHRISTIAN learns that by bright views of his love, mercy, and goodness, and by thoughts, desires, and hopes, God fills the hearts of Pilgrims with joy and gladness, and enables them either to go on their way rejoicing, or, in the hour of trial, to fight the good fight of faith, and firmly to press *onward*, patiently to look *forward*, piously to look *upward*, and vigorously to *contend for the truth* against all the unfruitful works of darkness. CHRISTIAN learns, moreover, from the experience of Christian warriors, who, like himself, are traveling to the celestial abode, that when fresh assaults are made against them, the recollection of past victories and the consciousness of the Divine presence will assuredly animate them for the conflict, and by the grace of God the victory will be theirs, and none shall be able to keep them from the path that leads to the Heavenly City.

The day of spiritual communion is closed by the retirement of CHRISTIAN to his rest and calm repose, within the safe enclosure of the chamber Peace. Here is perfect peace, in the household of faith—not in the midst of difficulty, as when he slept in the pleasant arbor, but in the midst of Christian fellowship, and under the roof where heavenly virtues dwell. Here was the Pilgrim safe; his person and his property, his garments and his credentials, all are safe; and that God who has been about his path, is now about his

---

*Count Zinzendorf, "Communion."

bed. This period of rest is that phase of Christian experience when the Christian man is withdrawn from beating storms, and roaring lions, and other unfriendly influences of the outer world, and lays him down in peace, and awakes refreshed, to face the duties and the dangers of the world outside.

The Study.—We must now follow the Pilgrim through the galleries and chambers of the Palace, for in Christian communion there are many things to be seen, and learned, and known, both in doctrine and example, in duty for the present, in preparation for the future, and in prospect of the final issue. Accordingly, the fair sisters first conduct the Pilgrim to the "Study." Here are contained the ancient records of the Lord of the Hill; and here his generation, his deeds, his followers—all are duly registered. Here also are the narratives of the bold, brave heroes of his army, the mighty warriors of the King, who have left their names emblazoned on the Book of Life, and their deeds engraven as with an iron pen upon the rock for ever. This is the place for the "students" of Divine knowledge.

The armory.—This was the basis of another day's instruction. Here was the receptacle containing the weapons of the spiritual warfare. All the parts of the Christian panoply—"the whole armor of God"—are supplied from this store-house. And there is no stint or sparing of the supply; yea, though the host should be as the stars of heaven for multitude, there is enough for each, and enough for all, and yet to spare. Out of these supplies was CHRISTIAN himself armed and equipped ere he departed from the Palace on his homeward way.

This armory, moreover, served as a museum, or treasury of those ancient implements of the good fight of faith, by which men in olden time did fight and win their spiritual battles. These relics—not for worship, but for remembrance, were evidences of the might of other days, when the strong champions of the Lord went in and out among their people, and were jealous for Jehovah's sovereignty, and avenged his righteous cause against all opposers. This was just such a treasury of ancient lore and deeds of faith as Paul supplies in the eleventh chapter of his Epistle to the Hebrews—that memorable record of men that lived and died in faith.

Immanuel's Land.—Who sees with the eye of faith, sees with a far-seeing eye. Not only within the chambers of the Palace, but also from the outer heights are prospects and perspectives of far-off scenes, and stages yet to be attained. Hence may be seen some of the great land-marks of the way: from the Palace Beautiful the Delectable Mountains may be seen in the distance; and by-and-by, from those Delectable Mountains will the Pilgrim see the gates of the Celestial City. Thus it is that Faith's wide prospect perpetually expands, and from successive stand-points more distant prospects dawn upon the sight. Faith

> "Leads from goal to goal,
> And opens still,
> And opens on the soul."*

To men of faith is the promise made—"They shall behold the land that is very far off," (Isaiah 33:17). That land is pleasant; even in the distant prospect presenting its vineyards and its woodlands, its fountains and rivers of waters. At this prospect the Pilgrim's zeal is quickened, and he desires to depart, that he may the sooner gain that goodly outpost of the City. But the journey lies through battle-fields; and through many a hard-fought fight is the issue to be attained.

They harnessed him.—Till now, the Robe received at the Cross is the raiment of the Pilgrim, and this continues to be his clothing. But besides this dress, he is accoutred with a suit of armor from the armory of the Palace. To what purpose this precaution was taken will ere long appear. He is now invested with armor becoming a Pilgrim-soldier of the Cross—the girdle of truth about his loins, the breastplate of righteousness, his feet shod with the preparation of the gospel of peace; besides all these, there are given to him the shield of faith, the helmet of salvation, and the sword of the Spirit; and there is added the weapon of All-prayer to these (Ephesians 6:14–18). Thus equipped, the Pilgrim is about to be committed to the onward stages of his journey.

To some purpose, indeed, was this sojourn in the Palace Beautiful. In very weakness he entered its portals; but now he is refreshed, comforted, instructed, edified, enlightened, armed, and strengthened. Having now tasted the blessings of Christian communion, he asks the porter at the gate whether any fellow pilgrims have passed by; and he is informed that one FAITHFUL has just passed on before him. This man has not enjoyed the Christian intercourse of the Palace, but shall by-and-by reap the benefits of CHRISTIAN'S company, as CHRISTIAN, in his turn, shall also enjoy the fellowship of FAITHFUL. "Iron sharpeneth iron; so a man sharpeneth the countenance of his friend," (Proverbs 27:17).

Then he began to go forward.—Not alone does he depart; for the

---
*Alexander Pope, "Essay on Man."

fair sisters bear him company to the foot of the hill. "The things that accompany salvation" form the escort of the Christian in all difficult places. Accordingly, as the Pilgrim has been enabled to climb the hill Difficulty at the one side, so he is assisted in his descent into the low-lying valley at the other side—the Valley of Humiliation. Oh, how hard it is to walk safely down that steep declivity! Flesh and blood resist the effort; but, assisted and accompanied by Divine virtues and graces, this may be accomplished, at least with safety.

> "Thus to the vale they all descend,
> Whither the Pilgrim's footsteps tend—
> A lonely dell.
> They give him of their goodly store,
> As emblems of the love they bore;
> And then—Farewell!"

CHAPTER IX.

APOLLYON.

INTRODUCTION.—How well proportioned to our need is the provision for the way! Our God and Father will not suffer us to be tempted, tried, or tested beyond that we are able to bear. He superintends the proportion of trouble and conflict that is laid upon his children, so that they be not surcharged or over-weighted. He has hitherto mercifully provided for the Pilgrim's welfare; and before difficulties arise, God has bestowed upon him strength, in anticipation of his need.

So is it now, at this stage of the journey. We have just seen the Pilgrim provided with weapons in the armory of the Palace Beautiful; and as a mailed warrior he has departed from that resting-place, which he had entered as a benighted traveler. We now begin to trace in the sequel the object and design of that strengthening counsel and refreshing communion of which he has been a partaker, while enjoying the privileged company of the Christian virtues that dwelt in that fair House. Forth from the Armory, and in full equipment, he is conducted by the fair sisterhood of the Palace down the hill—to the low-lying Valley of Humiliation.

Diverse are the experiences of pilgrims, even in the self-same stage of the pilgrimage. To CHRISTIAN the descent was "dangerous;" and the Valley (when he got there) became the battle-field of one of the fiercest encounters that fell to his lot in the course of his journey. Yet this Valley is not thus perilous to all pilgrims. In the Second Part of the Progress it is described as "a fruitful place"—"the best and most fruitful piece of ground in all these parts." It consists of meadow-land and green valleys, "beautiful with lilies;" filled with sheep, and resounding with the pastoral songs of the shepherds; and its chiefest glory is, that it was the chosen dwelling-place of Jesus, the Lord of all.

But to our Pilgrim it was a place of sore conflict. It appears, from the light of interpretation thrown upon it in CHRISTIANA'S pilgrimage, that CHRISTIAN had wandered into a dangerous part of the valley, called Forgetful Green; and that it was here he was exposed to the assault of the great foe, APOLLYON. As a general rule, these hard experiences from without answer to some weakness from within. But if we be forgetful of God, our God and Father is not forgetful of us. Hence the timely provision of armor—the panoply of God, the weapons of the warfare, bright and burnished; and ere long they will be needed.

> "Descending to the vale below,
> There's trouble on the way.
> Christian! prepare thy ready bow,
> And strength for this thy day!
>
> "Unsheath thy glist'ning, trusty sword;
> Thy spear bring forth with might.
> Pilgrim! be valiant for thy Lord,
> And God defend the right!"

Valley of Humiliation.—From the height of Christian privilege a descending path and a darkening prospect now lie before the Pilgrim. He that had gone *up* the hill, must now go *down* at the other side—down to the valley, the Valley of Humility; lower down—to the Valley of Humiliation; lower still—to the Valley of the Shadow of Death. Very timely, and in anticipation of his direst need, has been the provision and refreshment of the Palace Beautiful, and the conversation of its inhabitants. Now, through scenes of danger and of darkness, CHRISTIAN is appointed to pursue his onward journey.

The Valley of Humiliation is a deep, low-lying vale. The descent to it is both difficult and dangerous; but to dwell there is profitable to the spirit of pilgrims. It tends to the formation of, at least, one part of the Christ-like character, for Jesus had his dwelling there; and he who would be like to Christ, must be familiar with this humble and lowly portion of the Pilgrim's lot.

A foul fiend—Apollyon.—"And they had a king over them, which is the angel of the bottomless pit, whose name in the Hebrew tongue is Abaddon, but in the Greek tongue hath his name Apollyon."—Revelation 9:11. Here, then, the Allegory means to depict a conflict with the powers of hell, with Satan himself. It is one of those fierce assaults of the devil with which he seeks to recover his lost prey, and if not this, to destroy them. The name APOLLYON means "The destroyer."

The description of this monster is conveyed in a sentence that gathers into itself the accumulation of all those characteristics of

Satan that are most hideous and horrible, deadly and dangerous. The scaly leprosy of the old serpent covers APOLLYON as with a coat of mail. He had "wings like a dragon," to indicate the rapidity of his flight, and the ravages of his march; "feet like a bear," for softness of tread, and strength and power to injure; "fire and smoke" came forth from his nostrils, representing the inner fire that burns within the breast of the fallen angel, and his very breath tells of the fiery realm he rules, and the fiery wrath he wields; "his mouth as the mouth of a lion," the rampant, raging, roaring lion, seeking whom he may devour.

No armor for his back.—In the enumeration of the Christian armor in the armory (Ephesians 6:14–18), there is no mention of any protection for the back of the Christian warrior. The ancient Romans, and, indeed, all warlike nations, made no provision for the backs of their soldiers; for they said that the soldier who turned his back to the foe deserved no armor to protect him. The duty of a soldier is always to present a full front to the enemy; and therefore is he provided with breastplate and helmet, with sword and shield—armor offensive and defensive; but "no armor for his back." The duty of the Christian soldier is to stand and to withstand. This is the way to "resist the devil." It is in the spiritual as in the carnal conflict—retreat is danger; and to flee from the fight is the surest way to an ignominious defeat. This thought aids the Pilgrim, now standing in the path, to receive the first shock of the foul fiend APOLLYON.

Began to question with him.—Not first with a battle-shock, but with tempting questions. Thus did Satan with our first parents. By cunning conversation he gained their ear, and thence probed deeper, to the heart; and at last he won them by fair speeches and "well-placed words of glozing courtesy." Thus did he also with our Lord himself. He began not with the striving unto blood, as in the agony, but with cunning questions and with insidious arguments did he tempt the Lord. And even so he begins with us. He forbears to fight, if he can gain the conquest of a soul on lighter terms.

The commencement of APOLLYON'S onslaught upon CHRISTIAN is made in the form of a question, "Whence came you?" and by the answer to this inquiry he is emboldened to lay a legal claim to the allegiance of the Pilgrim. The City of Destruction is Satan's city, and he is its Prince; and accordingly he claims the Pilgrim as one of his subjects.

Thou hast already been unfaithful.—Here is Satan set forth in his true colors—as the "Accuser of the brethren." He tempts us to sin, that he may himself accuse us. But the Pilgrim answers him again, quoting the power and love of God in Christ. And as for the root of sin, that he ascribes to Satan, seeing it was implanted during the time of the bond service.

At this complete overthrow of his successive temptations, APOLLYON is wrathful; CHRISTIAN is resolute.

The description of this battle of the warrior with the powers of darkness has ever been considered as a master-piece of a master-mind. For vigor and spirit of detail, revealing the alternating fortunes of the fight, it stands as one of the best delineations of the real and earnest conflict the Christian soldier has to wage with Satan.

> "They said the war was brief and easy;
> A word, a look, would crush the throng.
> To some it may have been a moment's conflict;
> To me it has been sore and long."*

With real anxiety we view the quick dispatch of fiery darts from the quiver of APOLLYON, and the disastrous consequences—the many wounds of CHRISTIAN in head, and hand, and foot. We cannot be unconcerned for the result, when in the strife the Pilgrim falls, and in the fall he drops his sword. This suspense increases when we behold APOLLYON taking advantage of his opportunity, having the upper hand of his antagonist, while CHRISTIAN despairs even of his life. All now seems lost, the battle ended, and our Pilgrim well nigh carried off the field, the victim of the Destroyer. But at this point occurs the climax of the story, and its great spiritual lesson, too. The Pilgrim, being weak, is made to feel his weakness. Accordingly, it is while he is thus prostrate, and his hand cleaveth no longer to his sword, that the great fact of his weakness is brought home to him in all its dread reality; and the victim looks to the Invincible for strength, nor looks in vain; for Divine strength is made perfect in his weakness, and he grasps his sword again, and instantly the battle changes—APOLLYON is wounded with a deadly thrust, and spreads his dragon wings, and betakes himself to his dark prison-house. Meanwhile, CHRISTIAN, who is "more than conqueror," is left in possession of the field. And now, weary and faint after so great a struggle, he presents his thanksgiving to the God of battles. Taught by hard experience, he sheathes not his sword; but he addresses himself to his onward journey, prepared for every assault.

---

*Horatius Bonar, "The Good Fight."

CHAPTER X.

THE VALLEY OF THE SHADOW OF DEATH.

> "O Father-Eye, that hath so truly watched;
>   O Father-Hand, that hath so gently led;
> O Father-Heart, that by my prayer is touched—
>   That loved me first, when I was cold and dead:
>
> "Still do thou lead me on, with faithful care,
>   The narrow path to heaven, where I would go;
> And train me for the life that waits me there,
>   Alike through love and loss, through weal and woe!"[*]

INTRODUCTION.—These words of the German hymn may be adopted as a fitting embodiment of our Pilgrim's feelings, when, descending to a lower level than the Valley of Humiliation, he enters on the deeper Valley of the Shadow of Death, and begins to realize the darker experiences of that dreadful pass, where he was "worse put to it than in his fight with APOLLYON."

This Valley is a continuation of the preceding scene. Scarcely has the good fight been fought, when a horror of great darkness overcasts the vale, and gloomy terrors throng upon the Pilgrim's soul, and he walks that live-long night through a darkness that might be felt, and through spiritual antagonisms that intensified both the darkness and the danger. The whole scene—from the first assault of APOLLYON to the sun-rising in the valley—is a continued series of perils encountered, dangers avoided, and difficulties overcome, that seemed insuperable. It is the reproduction in allegory of Bunyan's own spiritual experiences, as more fully described in his "Grace Abounding." There he details the anxious travail of his soul, the dark days and wearisome nights that were appointed for him to pass through, during which his soul refused to be comforted, and all joy, and hope, and promise seemed as though they had departed; rendering his experience like to that of a spiritual death, casting its dark shadow over all his faith, and hope, and spiritual joy. He writes—"I fell, therefore, at the sight of my own vileness, deeply into despair;

---

[*]Karl Johann Philipp Spitta, "Our Father, Redeemer Guide."

for I concluded that this condition that I was in could not stand with a state of grace. Sure, thought I, I am forsaken of God; sure I am given up to the devil, and to a reprobate mind. And thus I continued a long while, even for some years together."

Another paragraph of this personal experience recalls more distinctly the scene of the Shadow of Death, with its increasing darkness, and swelling tides of anguish. He writes—"For about the space of a month after, a very great storm came down upon me, which handled me twenty times worse than all I had met with before; it came stealing upon me, now by one piece, then by another; first, all my comfort was taken from me; then darkness seized upon me; after which, whole floods of blasphemies, against God, Christ, and the Scriptures, were poured upon my spirit, to my great confusion and astonishment. These blasphemous thoughts were such as also stirred up questions in me against the very being of God, and of his only beloved Son; or whether there were, in truth, a God, or Christ, or no."

But all pilgrims fare not thus badly, even in this dark Valley; for, by-and-by, FAITHFUL reports his exemption from such dreadful experiences, both here and in the Valley of Humiliation, saying—"I had *sunshine* all the rest of the way through that, and also through the Valley of the Shadow of Death."

The Shadow of Death.—This must be understood as a season of rising doubts, and returning convictions, and dark surmisings as to one's spiritual state. It maybe called "Satan's hour and the power of darkness." APOLLYON, foiled in his direct personal assault upon the Pilgrim, now summons to his aid his legion of evil spirits.

I saw in my dream.—The Dreamer now sees the Pilgrim already entered on the dark Valley. He treads delicately a very narrow path, with danger pressing sore upon him on either side. Here are no "stepping-stones," as in the Slough. Yea, even a good man falling in here finds no foot-hold. All help and promise, all hope and rescue, must here be found in Christ—in Christ alone. "HE THAT IS ABLE" must pluck them out.

> "Lead, kindly Light, amid the encircling gloom,
>   Lead thou me on!
> The night is dark, and I am far from home;
>   Lead thou me on!
> Keep thou my feet; I do not ask to see
> The distant way; one step's enough for me."*

---

*John Henry Newman, "Lead, Kindly Light."

The mouth of hell.—He here speaks, perhaps, of that season of bodily and spiritual weakness alluded to in his "Grace Abounding," where he says, "Again, as I was at another time very ill and weak, all that time also the tempter did beset me strongly, for I find he is much for assaulting the soul when it begins to approach towards the grave; then is his opportunity, laboring to hide from me my former experience of God's goodness; also setting before me the terror of death and the judgment of God."

Amid these inward spiritual antagonisms, he found he must resort to inward and spiritual weapons. And accordingly his sword, with which he had defeated APOLLYON, is now sheathed; and the spiritual weapon of "All-prayer" must now be put in exercise.

But he abides in prayer; and prays all through the Vale of Death. And the great power of prayer is answered, for by it the fiends are held at bay. Yet this is the worst part of the pass—the crisis of the danger; for now the mind of poor CHRISTIAN is "confusion worse confounded," by reason of the inward suggestion of the Evil One, and the blasphemies that he hears uttered as from his own heart, and by his own voice. To this also he alludes in his "Grace Abounding"—"While I was in this temptation, I would often find my mind suddenly put upon it to curse and swear, or to speak some grievous thing against God, or Christ his Son, and of the Scriptures."

For several miles together.—By these measures of the Pilgrimage he means *days* and *years* of his actual experience, during which the Evil Spirit troubled him and did abide with him. Two such seasons in particular fell to his lot; and one of these continued as long as two years and a half. Thus was this man of God deeply exercised in his innermost soul. But God had a great work for him to do, and he must be disciplined and prepared to do it, even though it be through the fiery furnace.

He heard the voice of a man.—Not only the voice, but the comfortable words uttered tended to the renewal of the Pilgrim's joy and gladness. The voice was heard singing David's pastoral song (Psalm 23), and this was comfortable to CHRISTIAN—1. Because it was an evidence that he was not alone in the Valley. 2. Because it proved that Pilgrims could yet afford to sing cheerily and joyfully even in the Valley of Death; and, 3. Because a promise was thereby given that the Pilgrim may yet overtake his more advanced brother, and have the enjoyment of his company.

> "Christ, thou bright and Morning Star,
> Now shed thy light abroad;
> Shine on us from thy throne afar
> In this dark place, dear Lord,
> With thy pure, glorious word."

And by-and-by the day broke.—The night of weeping is ended; and a morning of joy appears. This tyranny is overpast. After midnight is far spent, the dawn of hope arises on the Pilgrim's soul. Ye tried and afflicted pilgrims, put ye your trust in God; he will not always chide, neither will he keep his anger for ever.

Pope and Pagan.—These are pictured as two giants—representatives of the power and tyranny of olden times, that held men bound, body and soul, in the bondage of ignorance and superstition.

The allusion here is to the cruelties that characterized the religion of the heathen, who dwelt in the habitations of cruelty; and to the persecutions waged by the Church of Rome against the saints and martyrs of the Church of God, who were bold to confess the faith of Christ crucified, and, in the face of fiery persecutions, counted not their lives dear unto them. These have been, indeed, two gigantic systems—the one overspreading the face of the world; the other defiling the face of the Church.

PAGANISM has reduced the Creator to the level of the creature; has degraded worship to idolatry, religion to superstition, revelation to mythology, and truth to fiction. In this, man has been the chief sufferer, spoiled of his true glory, robbed of his inheritance. His better nature has deteriorated into savagery and barbarism, into cruelty and hatred, into vice and sensuality. The finer feelings of the soul have been dwarfed and stunted in their growth. Charity, sympathy, gentleness, meekness, and all moral duties, are exchanged for physical force, treachery, torture, deceit, and guile. "And even as they did not like to retain God in their knowledge, God gave them over to a reprobate mind," Romans 1:28.

ROMANISM has been to the Church what Paganism has been to the world—a spoiler of men's faith, and a persecutor of men's lives. It has taken human nature as its guide, and, accordingly, has wrought out a religious system of curious and cunning work, incorporating much of the religion of the heathen with the religion of Christ, and striving by piecemeal and by development to make religion what man *would like it to be*, easy to flesh and blood; in a word, a human religion founded on that which is divine; human tradition superadded to revelation; carnal superstition joined to spiritual worship; mortals made mediators, in conjunction with, and ofttimes to the exclusion of, Jesus, the only Mediator between God and men. "Being ignorant of God's righteousness, and going about to establish their own righteousness, they have not submitted themselves unto the righteousness of God."*

Nor are these giants bereft of either life or power. Bunyan represents PAGAN as having been long since dead, and POPE as being sunk into a state of decrepitude and decay; and therefore the Pilgrim "went without much danger" past their cave. Bunyan seems to speak of their history *in this country*. PAGAN once held sway in Britain, but has long since ceased in the land; albeit he still lives and thrives throughout the larger portion of the globe. And POPE, although shorn of much of his strength at the period of the Reformation, and more particularly in this country, yet wielded the power of a vast dominion, in Bunyan's days as in our own, over the lives and liberties of men in other lands.

---

*Romans 10:3—For they being ignorant of God's righteousness, and going about to establish their own righteousness, have not submitted themselves unto the righteousness of God.

CHAPTER XI.

CHRISTIAN AND FAITHFUL.

INTRODUCTION.—The by-gone scenes of the Pilgrimage have been gradually increasing in interest, and have already well nigh culminated to a point; the reader (if it be a first reading) is perhaps anxious to know how the story is to be much further prolonged; or, if prolonged, how the interest can be sustained, seeing that such experiences as those of the preceding chapters can hardly be surpassed by any subsequent scenes. Here we are reminded of the words of Montgomery's essay on the Allegory; speaking of this new phase of the narrative, he writes:—"The author has displayed great skill in introducing a companion to his Pilgrim in this place. Thus far, the personal adventures of CHRISTIAN had been of the most extraordinary kind, and sufficient of themselves to exercise the reader's sympathy for him; but these feelings would have languished from weariness, however intensely the sequel might have been wrought, had attention been claimed for a solitary wanderer to the end of the journey. Here, then, the history, which has probably reached its climax in the preceding scenes, revives, by taking a new form, and exciting a fresh interest, rather doubled than divided, though two have thenceforward to share it instead of one. Besides, the individual experience of one man, however varied, would not have been sufficient to exemplify all the most useful lessons of the Gospel, unless the trials of many persons, of different age, sex, and disposition, were interwoven."

And not only is the interest of the story better sustained, but also the experimental value of the narrative is largely enhanced by the introduction of the character of FAITHFUL. This new personage opens out a new view of spiritual progress and experience, and sets before us a worthy and exemplary illustration of a consistent walk, and steadfast testimony, even unto death. It would be a profitable study, even to the most experienced Christian, to sit and listen to these men, CHRISTIAN and FAITHFUL, comparing notes of the way, contrasting or combining their respective experiences of the Pilgrimage, and proving in their own persons how "there are diversities of operations, but it is the same God which worketh all in all," 1 Corinthians 12:6.

New views of the Pilgrimage, new foes of the Pilgrims, new phases of temptation, and new features of resistance, are furnished to us in this part of the story. There are many who have never fallen so low, or risen so high, in spiritual experience, as CHRISTIAN did. FAITHFUL may, perhaps, better suit their case. While CHRISTIAN has been a deeply exercised man, severely tried, and so oft despairing, the career of FAITHFUL has pursued the more even tenor of its way, and is more equable than that of his fellow-pilgrim. It is therefore, perhaps, more assimilated to the ordinary experience of Christians. Let us, then, give earnest heed to FAITHFUL'S counsel, admonition, and encouragement!

A little ascent.—There are at times provided for the Christian stand-points, for purpose of observation, with a scope proportioned to the elevation. We remember the far-off prospect, as viewed from the heights of the Palace Beautiful; and now the Pilgrim, from "a little ascent," is enabled to see "a little in advance," but sufficiently far for his present requirement,—to discern his future companion, FAITHFUL, somewhat in advance of him. Such prospects as these are useful and helpful to pilgrims, sometimes near to, sometimes far off; at one time to reveal the outposts of the Celestial City, and at another time to present the view of a fellow-pilgrim, sufficiently near to be overtaken for sake of companionship.

"I am upon my life."—FAITHFUL seems to consider himself unsafe so long as he is not hasting on. Even on the Narrow-way he fears the pursuit of "the avenger of blood." There is a sense in which Christ, apprehended by faith, is our City of Refuge, even here; so that, if found in him, we are safe. And there is yet another sense in which heaven is our Refuge, and until we reach its safe harbor, and enter its open gates, we are not safe—fully or finally safe. In this latter sense FAITHFUL estimates his position, and therefore delays not, but speeds onward his way. We have already seen enough of the road to know that manifold and great dangers beset the pilgrims that walk thereon; and while there is all possible scope for faith, there must be no yielding to presumption.

Suddenly stumbled and fell.—FAITHFUL, though he has started later from the City of Destruction, yet has he gained the advance of his brother: "the last shall be first." And now CHRISTIAN overtakes and overruns his fellow, and, vain-gloriously priding himself on his advantage, he stumbled and fell: "the first shall be last." That vainglorious smile that played upon the lips of CHRISTIAN was the rising indication of the carnal nature still living and working in him; and, accordingly, this man, ever taught deep lessons by hard discipline, is by another fall taught a lesson of humility and watchfulness.

Had sweet discourse.—Fellow-pilgrims are allowed to bear each other company, so that they may entertain and encourage each other in Christian conversation: "They that feared the Lord spake often one to another," Malachi 3:16. The discourse of these men turns upon their experiences of the way. They had been fellow-townsmen in the City of Destruction, and are now fellow-travelers to the City of Zion. FAITHFUL, having started later than CHRISTIAN, is enabled to report the more recent intelligence of the doings of the citizens of Destruction. And, first of all, he reports that CHRISTIAN'S setting out on pilgrimage had caused an awakening and inquiry about his expedition, and the object of it. The majority talked disparagingly of his undertaking; but convictions were awakened in at least the mind of FAITHFUL, who, feeling that "Destruction" was not only destroying many souls, but was also itself to be destroyed, made haste to escape, and to follow as speedily as possible the example of CHRISTIAN. The example of a sinner forsaking sin and the associations of sin, is not without its effect upon those that are left behind. Such influences are felt, and often tend to bring forth blessed results.

In this conversation "neighbor PLIABLE" is also called to mind. We are informed of his return to Destruction, his reception by his old companions; their not very flattering opinion respecting him; and that he is now worse than if he had never set out at all.

Things that concern ourselves.—This is wise counsel of CHRISTIAN. Our disposition generally is, rather to talk of others, than look to ourselves; to speak of the failure of other men, rather than review our own progress. We are now enabled to read the records of a second pilgrimage, in the experience of a new Pilgrim, whose name is FAITHFUL.

In this review, it appears that FAITHFUL escaped most of the dangers that had befallen his friend, but had encountered other and different temptations and snares, which specially beset his own path. His progress to the Wicket-gate was, indeed, without the downfall of Despond, and without the intervention of WORLDLY-WISEMAN'S ill advice; and yet not altogether without danger, for one whose name was WANTON crossed his path, and sought to lure him into her net. There are many Pilgrims who would seek for the "steps" in Despond, and stoutly resist the plea of self-righteousness, who yet, through the weakness of their nature, would yield themselves to the winning ways and seductive influences of this temptation of the flesh, and thus fall away into peril more deep and miry than Despond.

In climbing this hill, a more easy and gentle service is offered by an aged man, whose grey hairs would, at first sight, seem to claim respect for his advice and counsel. This was ADAM THE FIRST—the old Adam, "of the earth, earthy"—whose service, and work, and wages are all carnal and corruptible.

FAITHFUL was enabled to resist the overtures of "the old man." But with what rending of the flesh and spirit is this parting made between the Christian and the old Adam! It needs a violent effort, and great grace withal, to be delivered fully from "the body of this death," And even then we are not wholly rid of his influence; for, moved with malice and hatred against us, he stirs up many a foe, and sends many a messenger of Satan to buffet us.

The place where the settle stands.—Here, again, their experiences meet, though in a different form. At the place where CHRISTIAN lost his Roll, FAITHFUL encountered another and different downfall. One, whose name was MOSES, overtook him, and dealt hardly with him—sharply, abruptly, severely, mercilessly. It is a brief scene, but eloquently instructive—a word, a blow; the Pilgrim falls; another blow, and he is as one dead; a plea for mercy, and in reply, not mercy, but another blow! This discipline of chastisement and wrath is stayed by the interposition of One who passed by.

There is no more telling or touching sentiment in the whole PILGRIM'S PROGRESS, than that which describes the marks by which this passing Stranger is recognized—"I perceived the holes in his hands and in his side!" It is but a single touch of the pencil, and lo, a complete picture stands before the eye, illustrative of the great truth,—"The Law was given by Moses, but grace and truth came by Jesus Christ." Bunyan well describes the power and wrath of the Law, where, in his treatise on "Justification," he writes—"As the Law giveth no strength, nor life to keep it, so it accepteth none of them that are under it. Sin and die, is for ever its language. There is no middle way in the Law. It hath not ears to hear, nor heart to pity its penitent ones." And in this remarkable scene he beautifully describes the power and grace of Jesus: by those wounds in his hands, and in his feet, and in his side, he delivers us from the Law.

He passes by, and bids the Law refrain, because those open wounds have satisfied all its weightiest demands upon the sinner, and present to us a better than a legal righteousness—the righteousness of God in Christ. "By his stripes we are healed."

I met one Discontent.—Such are some of the enemies we meet with on the road, who assault the citadel of the soul, and strive to take it, and dislodge the great Master that reigns within. There are also other enemies that are as thorns in the side of the Pilgrim, annoying and harassing him with a vexatious warfare. Of this latter class was DISCONTENT. He appeals to the temper and spirit of FAITHFUL, and is a type of a large class of men with whom we meet in the world.

DISCONTENT has succeeded in turning away many from the better land, by suggesting worldly motives, and proposing the objections of worldly minds. DISCONTENT meets many of us day by day. And as this kind of temptation is frequent, so the answer of FAITHFUL is important: he pleads a full and final break-off of kindred and acquaintance; and this severing of the ties of friendship is mutual— "they have disowned me, and I also have rejected them." He therefore has no more duties of friendship to perform towards them; nor can they now demand that he shall so shape his conduct as to please them. Their pleasures are not his pleasures now; nor are their ways his ways. He likes what they dislike; they hate what he loves.

I met with Shame.—It is not every Pilgrim that is appointed to meet the great APOLLYON in the Valley as CHRISTIAN did; but in the footsteps of FAITHFUL'S pilgrimage most of God's servants have trod, and are still called to tread. Many a man who is a hero in worldly things is but a very coward in spiritual things. Many a brave soldier, who would not hesitate to walk up to the cannon's mouth, is yet deterred from following Christ by the ridicule of his comrades. These weapons of shame have driven off many, who have consequently gone back, and walked henceforth in the paths of error and of evil.

Sunshine all the rest of the way.—With the last-named temptation, the earlier trials of FAITHFUL seem to have concluded; and for his consistency he is rewarded with clear sunshine to enlighten his path, where otherwise he would have been most exposed to danger and disaster—in the Valley of the Shadow of Death.

How diverse are the experiences of God's children! Sometimes through severity, and sometimes through gentleness (but in the severest discipline there is goodness still), are they led all the way to their journey's end. Where one man has darkness and devils to deal with, another has God's blessed sunshine to cheer him, His rod and his staff to comfort him. It is an alternating experience; not always darkness, nor always sunshine, but some of each; and, perhaps, each by turns. Thus it is that God leads his people: and his all-wise providence appoints the hard or easy, the joyful or the sorrowful, the bitter or the sweet. Today at Marah's bitter waters; tomorrow beneath the shade of Elim's palm trees.

> "So is it here with us on earth; and so
> I do remember it has ever been:
> The bitter and the sweet, the grief and joy,
> Lie near together, but a day between."*

---

*Horatius Bonar, "Marah and Elim."

CHAPTER XII.

TALKATIVE.

INTRODUCTION.—One of the distinguishing features of the PILGRIM'S PROGRESS is the rapid succession of characters that present themselves in the course of the Pilgrimage. We shall find that these characters are introduced, not only for ornament, but also for practical use. The purpose of the Allegory is not merely to draw grand pictures, but also to define true doctrine; and this doctrinal purpose is from time to time fulfilled in the conversations that are recorded, both of worthy and unworthy Pilgrims.

In the following scene, a man whose name is TALKATIVE joins himself to the Pilgrim. The experience of CHRISTIAN enables him at once to take the measure of the man, and to detect the hollowness of his profession. FAITHFUL is for a time deceived; he is even captivated by this "brave companion," who, to his mind, promises to make "a very excellent Pilgrim." And here commences one of those self-drawn pictures which are found at intervals throughout the narrative. The talkative professor is a type of a class of professing Christians. It has been said, "The deepest waters, are the most silent; empty vessels make the greatest sound, and tinkling cymbals the worst music."

Those readers of the Allegory who lightly pass over these conversational scenes are not able to enjoy the more picturesque pages of the story. These conversations are thrown in, for a great purpose—for the exposition of the true doctrines of the Gospel. The conversation that now ensues sets knowledge, and speech, and declamation in their right place, and lays the proper emphasis on the essentials of true faith—the *power* of religion, and the deep experience of saving grace in the soul. It further opens up the great difference between head and heart, between knowledge and action, between saying and doing, between words and works, between a dead and a living faith. Bunyan here rebukes the merely professional spirit of his own day. And in this he writes for every age. Alas! how large a measure of the same external religiousness prevails in our own times!

Whose name is Talkative.—The skill of the writer enables him to allow TALKATIVE to draw his own picture, and to represent his own character. And as he reveals himself, he is a mere flippant talker, a shallow professor.

To talk of the things of God.—This is the sum and substance of TALKATIVE'S idea of religion—"to talk." And the subject matter of his conversation further discloses the lack of heartfelt, experimental religion; for his topics are such as "history, mystery, miracles, wonders, and signs." These subjects, no doubt, are calculated to interest and instruct true Christian students, if, as FAITHFUL says, they are studied to the "profit" of the soul. But it is not with this view that TALKATIVE indulges in his wordy speculations. His object is simply to get, or, more likely, to display, "knowledge"—"striving about words to no profit, but to the subverting of the hearers."

To what length men may "talk" about religion, and how near they may, all the time, keep to the strict propriety of Christian conversation, appears from the circumstance that, till better informed by his more experienced brother, FAITHFUL was altogether deceived by the specious language of this talkative professor. FAITHFUL seems to have regarded him, not with suspicion, but with "wonder," and perhaps with admiration, when he thus lightly tripped along the whole permanent way of successive topics, upon which he was ready to discourse: anything on any subject, in heaven or on earth; on morals or religion; on secular or sacred things; on the history of the past, or the mystery of the future; on topics far off, or near home; on everything imaginable; on anything that anybody pleased! Truly, a very encyclopedia of spiritual knowledge was this man, TALKATIVE!

Christian modestly smiled.—That smile indicated CHRISTIAN'S better knowledge of the man, his shrewd idea that FAITHFUL had thus far been deceived, and that ere long he would discover his mistake. Indeed, this incredulous smile of CHRISTIAN'S at once produced an effect upon FAITHFUL, who expresses a desire to know more about his new companion. In this information, subsequently given by CHRISTIAN, new vigor is added to the description of the character of TALKATIVE. His family and his place of residence are both in keeping with his name and nature. These associations of the man are well put together by the writer of the Allegory, making up a complete picture of what Bunyan means to indicate under the name of TALKATIVE.

This man is no stranger to the words, "prayer," "repentance," "faith," "new birth," and such like. The words are found in his vocabulary; their sound is upon his lips; but there is not a particle of their inner spirit or power residing in his heart; "he knows but only to talk of them."

Empty of religion.—Whatsoever may be the pride of his bearing, the boastfulness of his professions, or the vanity of his words, he is discovered in all practical things to be utterly devoid of the power of religion. In his real self, in his secret heart, in his family circle, or in his social relationships, there is neither religious motive nor practice of religion. All the religion that is in him evaporates in words; and as example, like water, descends, so his children already begin to walk in the evil ways of their father. Dishonor is thus done to the sacred name and holy principles of true religion, through the insincerity and hypocrisy of those professors who "say and do not."

Foolish timorousness.—This is TALKATIVE'S more elegant synonym for "a tender conscience." The advice of this inward monitor, this law of God "written on our hearts," is reduced to the level of a vain alarm, a groundless fear. Surely, when men have accustomed themselves to speak familiarly of all the dread realities of religion, and with a mere lip-service to utter words on which eternity depends, conscience must be seared, and lost to all sense of the deep and eternal meaning of the words uttered.

Saying and doing are two things.—The words of the talker are belied by his works. Hence mere words without works to correspond, are but a dead letter, a body without the soul. It is to such a state of spiritual death St. James alludes, when he writes, "What doth it profit, my brethren, though a man *say* he hath faith, and have not works?" James 2:14. The Apostle here addresses those who talk of faith, but have nothing whereby to manifest it. And this is the great object of the present scene of the Allegory, as stated by Scott in his annotations:—"TALKATIVE seems to have been introduced on purpose that the author might have a fair opportunity of stating his sentiments concerning the practical nature of evangelical religion, to which numbers in his day were too inattentive; so that this admired allegory has fully established the important distinction between a *dead* and a *living* faith, on which the whole controversy depends."

The power of religion.—FAITHFUL is undeceived, and now perceives the character of his new companion. There is a spirit of rebuke observable all through CHRISTIAN'S dealing with TALKATIVE. He does not speak with him directly, but instructs his fellow-pilgrim how to probe the man's heart and conscience, and to expose his shallow pretence to piety, and thus either to reform him, or to get rid of his company altogether. Hence FAITHFUL is instructed to challenge the loquacious pilgrim "into some serious discourse about the *power* of religion." TALKATIVE soon displays his ignorance of the principles of vital religion, and then lays himself open to a series of personal inquiries as to the possession of religion in his own heart; whereupon, being sore pressed by the faithful questions of the Pilgrim, TALKATIVE loses temper, and ultimately separates himself from company so uncongenial to his own spirit and nature.

THE QUESTION.—A most important and essential inquiry is that now proposed by FAITHFUL—"How doth the saving grace of God discover itself when it is in the heart of man?" TALKATIVE is somewhat puzzled, but he has recourse to words, for all that; and proceeds to his divisions and subdivisions, until stayed in his flood of words by FAITHFUL, who will examine each point in succession.

A great outcry against sin.—This is the first of the marks of saving grace, as alleged by TALKATIVE. The sequel of the conversation will show how skilful was Bunyan, in thus interweaving in the Allegory so much of true doctrine as a corrective of that which is false. Here he shows that to *talk against* sin is not the same as to *depart from* sin.

Great knowledge, etc.—Knowledge is not salvation; but, if trusted to and rested in, it may be our condemnation. Knowledge of the Master's will is that thing that makes the difference between the "few stripes" and the "many stripes," according as it leads, or does not lead, to the doing of the deeds of duty.

THE QUESTION ANSWERED.—TALKATIVE has given unsatisfactory and insufficient answers to the searching inquiry of FAITHFUL respecting the discovery of saving grace in the soul. He has offered a "firstly," and a "secondly," and neither of these is correct. He is now challenged still further to define the marks and tokens of this indwelling grace. But he frets over his task, offended at the plain speech of FAITHFUL, and declines to render any further answer to his questions. Whereupon FAITHFUL undertakes to reply to his own inquiry.

The answer is twofold: Saving grace, in the *root* of faith, must be discovered to him that hath it; and, in the *fruit* of faith, it must be manifested to others.

The discovery of the gift of grace to one's own conscience is essential to a Christian man's peace and comfort. It is worthy of note, that the process of this discovery, as here described, follows the track of the Pilgrimage, as already traversed by our Pilgrim. Here, FAITHFUL is made to give expression to CHRISTIAN'S own actual experience:—1. Conviction of sin, with the heavy consciousness of impending wrath; 2. Sorrow and shame, confusion of spirit, and hasty flight; 3. The revelation of Christ, the Crucified One, as the Savior; 4. The necessity of closing with the salvation that is now offered in Christ; 5. The new nature with new appetites, hungering and thirsting after righteousness, which appetites are satisfied in communion with Jesus, and with his people; 6. In proportion to faith is the measure of joy or sorrow, strength or weakness—as in the Valley of Humiliation, and in the dark transit through the Shadow of Death. And with all these progressive signs and symptoms of saving grace, it needs a quickened power of spiritual vision and discernment, for these things are "spiritually discerned," 1 Corinthians 2:14. All these inward evidences, thus discovered and made known, constitute the witness of the Spirit with our spirit, that we are the children of God, Romans 8:16.

Do you experience this?—Do you? FAITHFUL has, indeed, dispatched the barbed arrow straight into the heart of TALKATIVE. The answer to such a soul-searching question must be given in the tribunal of conscience, and in the light of God's countenance.

Talkative began to blush.—This looks hopeful; but it proves too transient an effect to justify the existence of any abiding principle of good. TALKATIVE hardens into strong resistance, chafes over his discomfiture, calls his faithful monitor by opprobrious epithets, and provokes a still heavier censure, and a yet more personal reproof. "A fool's lips enter into contention, and his mouth calleth for strokes," Proverbs 18:6.

It is not every one that could bear this faithful dealing, and this outspoken speech. Men are not prepared to hear these withering admonitions; nor are they willing to acknowledge the likeness when depicted by the light of old Tell-truth. TALKATIVE is not able to endure the scathing speech of FAITHFUL, and, accordingly, he bids him adieu.

Rebuked, reproved, but not reformed, this loquacious professor has departed on his way. Occasion is then taken by the two Pilgrims (for CHRISTIAN has once more rejoined his fellow) to speak together upon this class of men, who assume the outer garb and guise of religion, and know nothing of its inner power. These are the men that do harm to religion; they encourage good hopes only to disappoint;

and give large promise of good, but only to fail of the fulfillment. As some one has said, "There may be much *head knowledge* where there is no *heart religion.*"

The subsequent conversation of the Pilgrims beguiles the way, as they walk and talk together. Their progress continues, and it is well they keep each other company, and enjoy the blessedness of Christian intercourse and fellowship. They have by this time advanced in their journey to a very desolate place.

CHAPTER XIII.

VANITY FAIR.

INTRODUCTION.—In the preceding chapter we left our Pilgrims traversing "a wilderness." There, though lonely, they would be comparatively safe, strengthening each other in Christian communion, and supporting each other in Christian faith and hope. But they are drawing near to an inhabited city—a city proverbial for its vanity, gaiety, profanity, and general forgetfulness of God, and disregard to his Word and Commandment. The name of this town is Vanity; and through it our Pilgrims are introduced to the scenes of Vanity Fair. Before committing them to these perils, a watchful Providence provides for them a timely admonition at the hands of EVANGELIST.

This episode of the narrative is intended to represent the world, in its earthly and fleshly character, with its business, and cares, and occupations, and pleasures, and sins, and sorrows, and its vanities in general; thus presenting a picture of the Christian man set in the midst of many and great dangers—*in* the world, but not *of* the world; his Christian consistency daily tried and tempted; his heart in danger of being wooed by carnal pleasure, and won to the side of vanity, and thus lost to the Kingdom; yet called to suffer for his attachment to the cause of Jesus. "Because ye are not of the world, but I have chosen you out of the world, therefore the world hateth you."—John 15:19.

Throughout this portraiture of the world in its opposition to the Church and people of God, Bunyan interweaves some striking illustrations of the working of the carnal mind, which is enmity against God. Some of God's people have passed through the Fair with scorn and contempt; some with danger to the body; all with danger to the soul; some with more, others with less of the world's opprobrium and neglect; some, through a fierce fight of affliction; and not a few through fiery persecutions, even unto death. The study of this stage of the Progress, its varied scenes, its characters, its circumstances, and its eventful issues, in their bearing on the sequel of the story, cannot but prove both interesting and instructive to any diligent reader of the great narrative before us.

My good friend Evangelist.—The two Pilgrims agree in owning EVANGELIST as their "good friend." He had discharged his kindly office in behalf of both; and it was through his advice and ministry that FAITHFUL, as well as CHRISTIAN, had been directed from the City of Destruction to the Wicket-gate. Hence their mutual salutations and friendly greetings. EVANGELIST is glad once more to meet those whose feet he has guided into the way of peace; and the Pilgrims are glad once more to hear the welcome voice, and to enjoy the profitable intercourse of one who has hitherto proved himself so good a friend and counselor.

This scene describes the heartfelt anxiety and longing of the true minister, respecting the progress and attainments of those who, through his ministry, have been brought to Christ. It also describes the affectionate attachment which binds him to the hearts of those who are his children in the Gospel. Thus the beloved disciple speaks—"I have no greater joy than to hear that my children walk in truth," 3 John 4.

How hath it fared with you?—These occasional re-unions of minister and people are designed for the purpose of review and retrospect, as well as of prospect and encouragement of hope. Intervals of time and absence sometimes leave large gaps in spiritual experience. In other cases, the interval is found to have been well filled up with progress in knowledge and experience.

So it was with CHRISTIAN and FAITHFUL. Their retrospect was one of thankfulness and praise to that God who had led them all the way, and filled their cup so full with his loving-kindness and tender mercies.

Right glad am I.—EVANGELIST is glad, as he afterwards testifies, for two reasons—"for my own sake and yours." Every minister has an interest in the results of the work of his ministry. It is possible for the spiritual builders to build up, not only "gold, silver, and precious stones," but also "wood, hay, and stubble," 1 Corinthians 3:12. The result will not be known here, but "the day shall declare it."

There is something touching, something thrilling, something of a melancholy interest, in this conversation between EVANGELIST and the Pilgrims. It reads very much like a parting address, in which the faithful minister commits his children to the future, and commends them to the care of the faithful Creator. A presentiment is awakened in our minds—a foreaugury of "bonds and afflictions;" and with a sad and uncertain spirit we follow the footsteps of CHRISTIAN and FAITHFUL, as, departing from the farewell of EVANGELIST, they contemplate in the distance the city of which they had been forewarned.

> "Methought I saw a city dazzling bright,
>   Where all were in pursuit of prospects fair,
> Of wealth, and fame, and many a proud delight,
>   That promised happiness, but led to care."

Vanity Fair.—This inimitable sketch of a world of pomp and pleasure, of sin and sorrow, of vanity of vanities, has ever been regarded as one of the chiefest and choicest scenes of the PILGRIM'S PROGRESS. It describes the emptiness of this vain world; the consistency of the Christian's walk; the estimate in which the Christian can afford to hold its best and choicest gifts and glories. But while men spend and are spent for the paltry and passing enjoyments of the world, the child of God is journeying to the better land, sitting loose to the things of time and sense, and looking only to the recompense of the great reward—the crown that is not of earthly glory, but "incorruptible, undefiled, and that fadeth not away."

Several rows and streets.—Bunyan interprets these to mean "countries and kingdoms." Seeing that the world is the Fair, the divisions and sub-divisions of the world would be represented by the streets and departments of the Fair. Hence Britain Row, French Row, and such like. And as each country and kingdom has its own peculiar vanities, and its own method of promoting the spirit of worldliness, so each is represented here as occupying a section of the Fair-ground, and contributing its merchandise to "vanity of vanities."

The ware of Rome.—This is specially mentioned, owing to the influence the Church of Rome had wielded in this country in former days, but which had so greatly diminished in Bunyan's time. "The blood, and bones, and ashes of men," which the Pilgrim had observed lying all around the cave of Giant Pope, would, perhaps, best represent the reason of the decline and discouragement of Rome's wares in England at the period when the Allegory was written.

The way to the Celestial City.—All Pilgrims must pass by this way. This is part of their probation, while they "seek a better country, that is, an heavenly." Here must their choice be made, here the profession of their faith, and their resistance to the tempting offers of the world. This is the place in which they are enjoined to "walk by faith, and not by sight." And, as men keep eternity in view amid the distractions of time, and desire the eternal weight of glory in preference to the phantoms of vanity, so shall they be made possessors of eternal things by-and-by. But this is for the trial of their faith.

Jesus once walked those streets, was tempted by those same vanities, had the offer of all the earth, and all its glory cast before his feet; and yet He, our Brother and our Friend, passed in sinless purity through all these temptations, "leaving us an example, that we should follow his steps," 1 Peter 2:21. If, then, we would walk in safety through Vanity Fair, we must walk in the strength of Jesus, who has overcome its great promoter, Satan.

Now these Pilgrims.—CHRISTIAN and FAITHFUL in Vanity Fair are intended to represent Christian men in the world—*in* it, but not *of* it. The world is to them a strange place, and they are to the world a strange people. The world knows them not, understands them not, loves them not. There is alienation and estrangement between the Christian and the world; and this is indicated by the (spiritual) raiment, speech, and spirit of the Pilgrims.

They are unlike not only in outward dress, but also in the inward adorning of a meek and quiet spirit—"all glorious within." The men of Vanity (did they but know it) are clothed in rags. Not one of them is clothed in courtly dress; nor is any prepared to stand before the King. They must first put off the world and the love of the world, and put on the robe which CHRISTIAN had received at the Cross—the spotless robe of a Savior's Righteousness.

They are also unlike in speech—not in the spoken dialect, but in the spiritual utterance of heart and soul, out of the abundance of which the mouth speaketh. Our words are the expression of our thoughts; and as the thoughts of the Christian man are renewed day by day, he speaks the corresponding words of holiness, so unlike the speech of carnal men. It is the Spirit that speaks, and not the lips only. "O Lord, open thou our lips, and our mouth shall shew forth thy praise!"*

They are, moreover, unlike in spirit—in the spirit of their love, their choice, and their desire. Their treasure was on high, and their heart was there also; or as Bunyan says—"their trade and traffic was in heaven."

But, the men being patient.—The spirit of Christian forbearance, meekness, and gentleness at all times exercises a powerful influence

---

*Psalm 51:15—O Lord, open thou my lips; and my mouth shall shew forth thy praise.

upon those that are without. There were those, even in Vanity Fair, who were moved to a spirit of sympathy for the Pilgrims, some fruits of which shall by-and-by appear. Notwithstanding their blindness and prejudice, they can yet perceive and appreciate the contrast between the persecutors and the persecuted. Even the ungodly can at times be persuaded, when by observation of Christian meekness and forbearance, they "take knowledge of us that we have been with Jesus." The consistency of these men, in spirit and in doctrine, tends to divide the multitude, and thus breaks the force of the opposition raised against them.

Finding that they could prevail nothing against these men, but that rather a tumult was made, the men of the Fair are impelled to yet more vigorous measures in order to suppress the protest against it by the Pilgrims. Their bondage is now made bitter to them, and the iron enters into their very soul. It is in that "cage" or prison of Vanity Fair that Bunyan now writes his narrative; and as he looks around upon his bondage, and looks within, to search out the cause thereof, he reads in his own experience, and in that of many of the tried and suffering members of Christ, this and the following scenes of the "Progress."

How descriptive is the whole picture rendered by the names of the respective parties who rise in opposition to CHRISTIAN and FAITHFUL. Each man's name speaks its own and is the very personification of some spiritual or earthly form of the antagonism of the world to the Church and people of God.

The circumstances of Bunyan's days, that gave a special point and power to his Allegory, are now past and gone; but the reality remains.

Envy.—This witness still continues to accuse the men of God. Envy is that spirit of the evil mind which calls religion a mere plausible fiction, and, through loyalty to Mammon, scoffs at "the principles of faith and holiness," and moreover, would blend into one element the realities of religion and the vanities of Vanity Fair. The true Christian cannot accede to this unholy combination.

Superstition.—This is also an element of accusation still urged against the true Christian. It means more than is implied in the ordinary use of the term. It includes all that formal worship which is opposed to the service of true faith.

Pickthank.—This is a suggestive name, and partly tells the nature of the man. He is a person who gathers what merit he can by volunteering evidence against faithful men.

To instruct you in our law.—The presiding judge delivers his charge to the jury. This charge is based on precedents, all of which directly tend to an adverse verdict, and seem to call for the extreme penalty of the law. "The tender mercies of the wicked are cruel;" and so the people of God have ever found it to be, when the civil power has sanctioned the sword as a weapon of persecution. Bunyan ably illustrates the continued enmity of the world against Divine faith. The spirit of intolerance needs but power, to wreak its vengeance on all who love the Lord Jesus in sincerity and truth.

The jury.—This is a keen satire on the judgment of this world when pronounced against the servants of God. The names of the twelve men are suggestive of all the elements of the carnal mind that go to make up the "enmity against God." Each of these, for some secret and personal reason, hates the light, and, if possible, will extinguish it.

Here is a formidable catalogue of vices arrayed against the Pilgrims of Sion. Each contributes his individual opinion in the direction of his own sin, and to the extinction of the protest in the person of the man of God. As Ahab dreaded the presence of Elijah—"Hast thou found me, O mine enemy?" (1 Kings 21:20), or as he feared Micaiah, the son of Imlah—"But I hate him; for he doth not prophesy good concerning me, but evil," (1 Kings 22:8)—so are all the opinions set against FAITHFUL, and all are gathered into the final verdict—"Guilty of death."

Thus the power of evil triumphed that day in Vanity Fair. But it was a short-lived triumph. "Stand still, and see the salvation of God!"

Thus came Faithful to his end.—His consistent protest conducted him to a martyr's death, and to the Christian's crown. In the working out of the story, CHRISTIAN is spared; but FAITHFUL forfeits his life as a sacrifice to the malice and wickedness of the men of Vanity.

But that "end" is to be viewed in a double light: in this world it was the triumph of an evil cause; the pain and agony of a protest, even unto death; the removal of one of God's people from a world that was not worthy of him; a type of the many persecutions, bodily and spiritual, that fall to the lot of the Church of God on earth. But there is also another and more blessed view. Here was Jesus suffering in the person of one of his members; a bold, unflinching protest, striving even unto blood; a seal set to the faith of FAITHFUL, proving its substance and reality; the shortening of a pilgrimage, and a more immediate entrance into the Celestial City. Here was the triumph of a faithful soul, caught up in a fiery chariot to the skies; a bright example and encouragement to those who thought as he thought, and believed as he believed; a seed that is destined, ere long, to bring forth fruit in the accession of a new comrade.

> "A moment's space, and gently, wondrously,
>   Released from earthly ties,
> The fiery chariot bears him up to Thee,
>   Through all those lower skies,
> To yonder shining regions,
>   While down to meet him come
> The blessed angel legions,
>   And bid him Welcome Home!"*

---

*Johann Matthäus Meyfart, "Jerusalem, Thou City Fair and High."

CHAPTER XIV.

CHRISTIAN AND HOPEFUL.

INTRODUCTION.—Once more the scene changes. FAITHFUL, whose ripened experience has already so tended to our instruction, has been withdrawn from the pilgrimage, and is "at rest." But, as it were out of the ashes of the martyr, another Pilgrim arises, to join himself to Christian, and to share the subsequent joys, and sorrows, and spiritual vicissitudes of the journey, even to the end. This man's name is HOPEFUL.

It is said that "the blood of the martyrs is the seed of the Church;" and so the noble and manly testimony of FAITHFUL, throughout all the trying scenes of Vanity Fair, has attached to his cause at least one illustrious convert, who now goes forth upon Pilgrimage. The mantle of the dying servant of God has fallen upon one who now succeeds him in the story, and ably sustains the thrilling interest of the narrative to its close.

It will be observed that this new Pilgrim fulfills quite a different phase of the pilgrimage. HOPEFUL is not represented as having passed through the Wicket-gate, as CHRISTIAN and FAITHFUL had done. Nor does he accomplish any of the preceding experiences of the way, but starts direct from Vanity Fair, and attaches himself immediately to the brotherhood of CHRISTIAN. In this, it is agreed on all hands, the Allegory is defective; but the exigency of the story requires it to be so. The consistency of the narrative, however, is not compromised by this; for, in an after-stage of the pilgrimage, we shall be conducted through a review of the spiritual exercises and experiences of HOPEFUL, from his first convictions to his ultimate conversion—all tending to illustrate the true meaning of the "brotherly covenant" into which he entered with CHRISTIAN, and which, as Mr. Scott remarks, "must be supposed to imply the substance of all that had been spoken of as necessary for final acceptance."

In these two successive companionships of our Pilgrim, it would further appear that Bunyan designed to indicate the perfecting of the Christian character—in Faith and Hope. As in the communion of FAITHFUL the Pilgrim's faith was deepened, so in the association of HOPEFUL, his hope was quickened. This is yet further opened up in the details of the story: through his intercourse with FAITHFUL, he has more thoroughly learned the great principles of Christian faith and the power of Christian consistency; and in his after-intercourse with HOPEFUL, he must pass through regions of Despond, and under the iron hand of grim Despair, and thus be taught wherein must rest the true hope of the children of Sion.

Christian went not forth alone.—We have already found, in the preceding chapter, that the wrongs and indignities inflicted upon CHRISTIAN and FAITHFUL, in Vanity Fair, and their patient endurance of the same, had won over to their side a certain number of the citizens. Of these some have ultimately ripened into true pilgrims of the road to Sion; but one in particular is now represented as accompanying CHRISTIAN on his way. The influence of good men is never wholly wasted; many seeds may perish in the soil, but some will yet supply sheaves for the reaper, so that "he that soweth and he that reapeth may rejoice together."* The protest of these Pilgrims, concluding with the martyrdom of FAITHFUL, has now added one new convert to the faith of Christ and to the path of the pilgrimage.

Whose name was Hopeful.—A well-chosen name, especially as the successor of FAITHFUL. Faith first, and then Hope; first the groundwork, then the superstructure. We are here for the first time introduced to one who ever after proves a meet companion and profitable help to CHRISTIAN, amid all the changing scenes of their chequered course.

A brotherly covenant.—Much is meant to be included in this expression. He has forsaken all for Christ; and in the strong confidence of believing faith he has attached himself to the Pilgrim of Sion—"Whither thou goest, I will go; and where thou lodgest, I will lodge: thy people shall be my people, and thy God my God."†

One, whose name was By-ends.—The narrative of HOPEFUL has scarce begun, when it is interrupted by the intervention of other pilgrims. We are introduced to new characters on the road, and to new experiences of the ways of men. Bunyan frequently groups his characters, and summons them before us in a way suggested by the

---

*John 4:36—And he that reapeth receiveth wages, and gathereth fruit unto life eternal: that both he that soweth and he that reapeth may rejoice together.
†Ruth 1:16—And Ruth said, Intreat me not to leave thee, or to return from following after thee: for whither thou goest, I will go; and where thou lodgest, I will lodge: thy people shall be my people, and thy God my God.

different stages of the journey. Thus, while yet in the vicinity of Vanity Fair, the Pilgrims meet with certain vain and worldly-minded men, who linger about its suburbs. These characters are introduced in order to exhibit, in this context, how the love of the world hinders men from running the Christian race.

First among this group is BY-ENDS. The character of this style of man is most strikingly delineated in his name, his origin, and his acquaintances. The town of Fair-speech, its great wealth and luxury, the characteristic names of its nobility and gentry, constitute a well-wrought picture of Bunyan's own times. The spiritual indifference and apathy of Mr. SMOOTHMAN, the double-mindedness of Mr. FACING-BOTH-WAYS, and the neutrality of Mr. ANY-THING, form a comprehensive picture of a generation utterly devoted to worldliness.

Mr. TWO-TONGUES, "the parson of the parish," is another touch of the pencil, conveying by a single stroke the character of many of the clergy of that period.

The rules adopted in the family of BY-ENDS are consistent with all other characteristics of the race. These worldly-wise professors always contrive to go with the stream, not against it. The purest days of the Church's history have ever been the days of her bitterest persecution. "What is the chaff to the wheat" in those days?—Jeremiah 23:28. Adverse wind and tide are for the trial and victory of the faith of good and true men; while the genial warmth of worldly pursuits encourages the growth of tares amid the pure grain.

Three men following Mr. By-ends.—A group of men of fleshly mind is now formed, by the accession of three persons, each and all bearing very significant names, and bound together by very characteristic associations. The design of Bunyan is still to bring his power of satire to bear upon the too prevalent sin of his age—the hypocritical profession of religion along with an essentially carnal mind and world-loving spirit.

The Christian man knows that these carnal things are but for a time, and that the interests of religion and the soul stretch away into Eternity; and therefore whether it be contempt or applause, his mind is still set on heavenly things; and, with the Apostle, he is ready to say—"I reckon that the sufferings of this present time are not worthy to be compared with the glory which shall be revealed," Romans 8:18.

Here, then, is a company of carnal men, who, through all sorts of by-ways and by-ends, contrive to hold the world, and love their money, and save all they can. Their calculations exhibit the groveling earthliness of their minds. The worldly-wisdom, the plausible speech, and the seeming prosperity of these men's counsel need only be interpreted in the light of God's word, and weighed in the balances with eternal things, to expose their vanity, their folly, their worse than madness.

Then said Christian.—Our Pilgrim's answer is based on precedents and examples found in Holy Writ, which prove how earthly gain may be changed to heavenly loss. 'Tis true, God ofttimes smiles upon the earthly career of good men, and blesses them with increase, and fills them with all manner of store and plenty; but it is quite another thing for a man to make religion a "stalking-horse to get and enjoy the world." CHRISTIAN, in his answer, well describes this to be but a reproduction of the carnal policy of the heathen against Israel, which God permitted to be signally outwitted and overruled.

A delicate plain, called Ease.—It is not all hard-going with the Pilgrims of Sion. There are times of refreshing, and in the midst of toil there are intervals of ease. These are generally timed according to the need of the way-farers of the road. And so now, after the hardships and bitter experiences of Vanity Fair, and the still further interruption of their onward course by the obtrusive companionship of BY-ENDS and his comrades, our Pilgrims are permitted to tread the soft and delicate glade called Ease. This oasis in the desert was narrow, and extended but a very brief space. Ease is granted to pilgrims, but only for a little time, and for present and passing necessity; and this necessity being answered, they must again take the road, and bear its flints, and endure hardness as good marching soldiers of the heavenly King. It is not well for pilgrims to sit too long "at ease in Sion." And soon, recruited and refreshed, they must up and away for the onward journey. So our Pilgrims, entering on the plain of Ease, "were quickly got over it." And as this refreshment was for compensation of the past, so is it also designed as a preparation for a danger soon to come.

A little hill, called Lucre.—This introduces the scene of the "Silver Mine," and its lurking dangers, and the deceptive voice of DEMAS—a name interwoven here, illustrative of the Apostle's words—"Demas hath forsaken me, having loved this present world," 2 Timothy 4:10. Whether *that* Demas did thus seek afterwards to beguile the members of the Christian Church, we are not informed; but the name is not unfitly given to this man, who now invites the Pilgrims to the Silver Mine.

Observe, this mine is said to be "a little off the road," and Pilgrims are asked "to turn aside hither." The scene therefore represents the undue pursuit of wealth, the going out of one's Christian course to seek after lucre—the very spirit of worldly love that prompted the Apostle's former companion to forsake the way of the Lord.

This is a tempting snare in the highway. It has charms already to win over the heart of HOPEFUL. Well was it for this new beginner that his more experienced brother, CHRISTIAN, was there to counsel him and thus to enable him to resist the tempting invitation of DEMAS. "My son, if sinners entice thee, consent thou not," Proverbs 1:10. CHRISTIAN'S resistance to temptation is, as on other occasions, accompanied by a rebuke of the tempter. He reminds this man of his spiritual pedigree, and how near of kin he is to the deception of Gehazi and to the treachery of Iscariot. Thus DEMAS is rebuked, HOPEFUL is instructed, and our good CHRISTIAN is again triumphant.

The anticipations of HOPEFUL respecting BY-ENDS and his fellows are fully realized. They saw the bait, and caught at it, and were drawn into the snare. The curtain here falls upon an unfinished scene—what became of these men is not told, but, suffice it to say, "they never were seen again in the way."

Where stood an old monument.—This stage is full of admonitory lessons; all tending to impress the great truth—"Let him that thinketh he standeth take heed lest he fall." Here is a memorial of ancient times, a standing witness of the lack of patience in running the race, a monument of one who set out upon pilgrimage, and looked back, and that "last fond look" became her ruin. The whole story of this monument is told in its inscription—"Remember Lot's wife."

The sight of this memorial on the wayside is "seasonable." It tends to justify CHRISTIAN'S recent advice to HOPEFUL respecting the Silver Mine. It also furnishes a timely admonition in advance of dangers yet to come—admonition that is much needed, as the sequel will shortly prove. It is a witness, too, set up full in view of the tempting snare beside which DEMAS stands; and thus it is, that against light and against knowledge, in spite of caution and example, men are drawn aside by worldly lust, and turn away from the path of righteousness, and never enter into rest!

Thus are we enabled to see the different kinds of destruction that fall upon men, for different reasons, and at different stages of the journey. There are some who continue in the City of Destruction, and shall be destroyed there in the overthrow of the city. There are others who, having set out, will still linger and look back; and, though half way toward Zoar, shall be turned into monuments of wrath. It is thus that men do ofttimes perish—not in the overthrow of doomed cities, not in the multitude of the ungodly; but alone, in their very flight, in their lingering love for the things they have left behind; as Israel looked back and longed after Egypt, and "their carcasses fell in the wilderness."

CHAPTER XV.

DOUBTING CASTLE AND GIANT DESPAIR.

INTRODUCTION.—The path of the Christian Pilgrims is laid through a varied country—through ups and downs, through hills and hollows, through night and day, through twilight and shadow, through sunrise and sunset, through clouds and darkness, through all sorts of diversified experiences—through all the manifold phases of spiritual life. A remarkable illustration of this character of the pilgrimage occurs in this chapter—ranging, as its narrative does, from the sweet refreshment of the "River of God," and the cool shade, and pleasant fruits, and healing leaves of its goodly trees, to the gloomy dungeon of Despair and all its dread associations. A bright morning of spiritual enjoyment merges into a day of danger, and through a darkening twilight sets in the very midnight of despair.

This is a well-wrought scene. The Pilgrims are parted from the refreshing water by a slight divergence of the path. The journey does not always border on the margin of the River of God. There are times when, for the trial of our faith, we must march among stony places, and feel the flints sharp and rough beneath our feet. This is the period of the journey at which By-path Meadow presents itself, and tempts the unwary. The spirit of Vain-confidence beckons them across the stile, to the tender grass, soft to the tread, and generous to the footsore and weary Pilgrims. The seeming parallel deceives even the experienced eye of CHRISTIAN; and by-and-by both CHRISTIAN and HOPEFUL find themselves hopelessly involved in darkness, and tempest, and other dangers; and in the midst of their dread alarms they fall asleep.

They are awakened by the rude grasp of a grim giant, whose name is DESPAIR, and whose dwelling-place is Doubting Castle. Here is a description of that fierce spirit of desperation which Bunyan had felt more than once in his own experience, and which still at times darkens the hopes, and clouds the light, and eclipses the sunshine of some of God's children. In the scene of Doubting Castle is described the agony of the doubting, desponding, despairing soul, from which all the comforts of the sweet, sustaining promises have fled away, and no light appears to guide the dark spirit back again to its lost peace, and joy, and hope. Some departure from the beaten track, some yielding to temptation, some seductive by-path has, at first imperceptibly, and at last but too surely, conducted the heedless steps of the Pilgrims into the dungeon of Doubt and into the darkness of Despair, so that with the Psalmist they say—"I am shut up, and I cannot come forth," Psalm 88:8.

Yet even here the Lord doth visit his people, and he releases them with the Key of Promise. Yes, the good promises of God open the iron doors of Doubt and the complicated locks of Desperation. The Promises penetrate through stone walls and bars of adamant, and administer their kind relief to many a doubting and despairing soul. The Star of Promise is the dawn of day; the Word of Promise is the Faithful Witness; the Key of Promise is as the key of David, that openeth and no man shutteth, and shutteth and no man openeth. To magnify this mighty deliverance are these dark experiences delineated here.

The river of God.—Once more are the Pilgrims comforted. The way-side dangers and temptations have been surmounted; profitable lessons have been learned; and now they need the comforts of the Spirit to refresh their soul. Accordingly, they are now led beside the still waters of comfort, beneath the grateful shade of the leafy trees which grow by the river-bank, and bear all manner of fruits, for food and medicine. This is a pleasant land; a land of meadows and green pastures, of fruits and flowers,

> "Where peaceful rivers, soft and slow,
> Amidst the verdant landscape flow."*

Here they might lie down safely.—So they lay down and slept. All places are not sleeping-places for pilgrims; but beside the river of God, and surrounded by the comforts and consolations of the Spirit, they may lay them down in peace, and take their rest. This was a place of high festival, a feast of fat things, a season of special privilege. And it is well that such seasons are accorded. They come like sunshine after rain, and sometimes in advance of danger, like the opportune provision made for the prophet, when the angel touched him, and said, "Arise and eat; because the journey is too

---

*Joseph Addison, "The Twenty-Third Psalm."

great for thee," 1 Kings 19:7. And it was well that our Pilgrims did thus eat and drink, for in the strength of that food they must go yet many days.

The river and the way parted.—The path does not continue parallel to the river-bank all the way; nor is it always covered with the grassy mead. There are times of withdrawal from the refreshing waters, when faith again is tried, and is still put upon probation. If pilgrims had their own way, they would, no doubt, build themselves tabernacles in the pleasant places of the pilgrimage; but no; "they are not yet at their journey's end;" and once more they must endure hardness.

As the path diverges from the river, it becomes rough and rugged. Seasons of comfort give place to seasons of trial; and they that have gone softly must now bear the flints, and patiently endure the ruggedness of the road. This is hard for flesh and blood to bear; and the natural man sighs after an easier lot and a fairer heritage.

A meadow and a stile.—This field was not the meadow of the river-bank. It was By-path Meadow. A stile separates it from the beaten track, so that the Pilgrims must go somewhat out of their way in order to pass from the one to the other. Their impatience of the road, and their desire for ease, surprised them into this divergence, and the tempting nature of the meadow-land deceived them. They saw its beginning, but they did not see its destination. Thus does the tempter blind our eyes. The moss-grown meadow, with its pleasant path and its seeming parallel, entices the Pilgrims from the road, and becomes the beginning of sorrows.

He went to the stile to see.—There is danger in a too close inspection of temptation. These Pilgrims stoutly resisted the invitation of DEMAS to go and see the Silver Mine; but now, at the suggestion of his own heart, CHRISTIAN must needs go and see this By-path; and, in going and seeing, he falls into the snare, and misleads his brother also.

Vain-Confidence.—This indicates the spirit that prompted the Pilgrims to so willful a departure from the right way. When Vain-Confidence assumes the leadership, and is followed, there is certain danger, and an inevitable downfall must ensue. Vain-Confidence persuades men contrary to their better teaching. They *wish* to escape the toil and travail of the road. Their practice then takes the direction of their wishes; their prejudice perverts their judgment; they lean to their own understanding; and ere long they reap the consequences.

Where are we now?—HOPEFUL had gently cautioned CHRISTIAN as to the possible danger of this departure from the way. He has had his misgivings all along, and is now the first to break the ominous silence of the scene—"Where are we?" Yes; it was dark, and danger lay ahead, and into that danger their false leader has already fallen, beyond their vision, but within their hearing. Here CHRISTIAN is the more guilty of the twain, and he sorely feels his folly and his sin; and feels it all the more acutely, because, through his ill advice, another is involved in peril. And yet it is from HOPEFUL he receives the consolation of the moment; for, true to his name, he is enabled, in the hopefulness of his heart, to see through the danger, and even ventures to believe "that this shall be for good."

They fell asleep.—It seems strange that they should thus have slept in the midst of such deadly peril. This is the reaction of the soul, wearied by its transgression, and worn out by the subsequent conflict with the storms, and tempests, and buffetings of conscience that pursue the transgressor to the very precincts of doubt and desperation. There is such a thing as settling down at ease in the midst of danger; the lulling of the conscience into peace when there is no peace; the encouragement of the spirit of slumber on the very borders of despair. Who shall awake the sleepers?

Doubting Castle—Giant Despair.—What a progression of disaster! From the easy stile and tempting meadow-land, through the by-path of an unbidden departure from the road the Pilgrims go on from bad to worse, until they find themselves in the strong captivity of Doubt, and under the grinding tyranny of DESPAIR. CHRISTIAN had seen a representation of this spiritual woe in the Iron Cage in the Interpreter's house; he had experienced much of its gloom and misery in his own person in the Vale of Death; and now he is appointed to pass through another season of horror and great darkness in the dungeons of Despair, aggravated by the thought that he and his comrade had but themselves to blame for the transgression which had brought them there.

This is a phase of spiritual experience that Bunyan had felt in his own person; and one that is also felt by many who are brought by willful sin and disobedience into these low depressions of conscience. This is a season of spiritual hunger, without any spiritual food; of spiritual thirst, without any of the waters of life; of spiritual darkness, without a single ray of heaven's own light; of spiritual loneliness and bondage, without company or communion of Christian men. Marvelous contrasts to the peace and blessedness of the morning of that day, by the waters of comfort and the fruits and flowers of the meadow-land!—

> "Yet clouds will intervene,
> And all my prospect flies;
> Like Noah's dove, I flit between
> Rough seas and stormy skies."*

Diffidence.—This was the Giant's wife: too gentle a name, perhaps, for one who proves herself to be as harsh, as cruel, and as unrelenting in her wrath as Giant DESPAIR himself. Dr. Cheever very well observes that "Mrs. Diffidence ought rather to have been called Dame Desperation, or Desperate Resolution; for she seems, if anything, the more stubborn genius of the two."

The night season is that selected for the counsels of DIFFIDENCE and DESPAIR concerning their treatment of the Pilgrims. It is in the hours of darkness that the sorrows of the soul are most intense, and the spirit of despair takes a more vigorous grasp of the troubled conscience; just as, on the other hand, it is in the hour of sunshine "the sunshiny weather" that Giant Despair is reft of his strength and spoiled of his power; and opportunity is thereby allowed, in the interval, for the friendly counsels of CHRISTIAN and HOPEFUL.

Brother, what shall we do?—Gloomy and dark thoughts fill the mind of CHRISTIAN. He seems harder put to it here than ever before. He broods over the suggestions of DESPAIR, and meditates release by untimely and unbidden means, even by his own hand—by suicide. How the man must have been possessed of the spirit of Despair, under the galling yoke of doubts that would not be solved, and of desperation that would not be comforted!

HOPEFUL'S answer to his brother was worthy of the man. He, the younger and the weaker of the two, is now the adviser of better things and the counselor of better purposes. He first dissipates these thoughts of self-murder, and will not permit them to be entertained at all. God's law, self-interest, and future judgment—all cry out against the cowardice of the man who flees as a fugitive from life, and presents himself unbidden at the bar of God. This point gained, HOPEFUL even ventures to lift the dark curtain, and to picture the possibility of a bright prospect beyond: the Giant may die, or may sometime forget his prey, or may abate his watchful vigilance, and thus leave a way of escape open to them. Such are ever the comforts of Hope in the very darkest moments of Despair.

---

*James Montgomery, "At Home in Heaven."

The conflict, however, continues; the darkness is as yet unrelieved by the dawn of light. CHRISTIAN falls again beneath the frenzy of the Giant, and meditates once more the surrender of self, and life, and all, at his suggestion. HOPEFUL again comes to the rescue! This time he tries the power of retrospect, and bids his brother call to mind the days of the past, and the scenes of his by-gone triumphs, and still to play the man. Heroes that have fought and won great battle-fields must not thus lightly allow themselves to be overcome. The hero of the Valley of Humiliation, who fought against APOLLYON, and prevailed; that patient Pilgrim who trod every dark step and dared every dangerous pass of the Shadow of Death; that valiant heart that scorned the dangers of Vanity Fair, and uttered his protest in the face of fire and fagot—surely, he knows better how to fight than thus cowardly to yield! Ay, and even by comparison with himself, doth HOPEFUL rally his despairing comrade—Thou strong man and brave warrior of the Cross, behold *me*, a weaker man than thou art! I too am wounded, weary of the strife, hungry, thirsty, dark, and comfortless as thou; and yet withal I am thy comforter—preaching to thee that thou shouldst live through this deep sorrow, and outlive this anxious struggle, and continue in the spirit of patience and endurance to the end! Brave words, good HOPEFUL, and yet braver deeds, thou man of God! He speaks out of his own darkness and dread uncertainty, and yet he speaks in words of comfort and in the fullness of his hope.

> "I know not what may soon betide,
> Or how my wants shall be supplied;
> But Jesus knows, and will provide!"*

Thus the tide of Despair is stayed, and all the threats of Doubting Castle are held at bay. HOPEFUL stands in the gap, and stays his desponding brother. The continued resistance of the Pilgrims now further provokes the angered spirit of the Giant, and he seeks by more demonstrative efforts to drive them to destruction. In the castle-yard are the bones of former victims of DESPAIR. The Pilgrims shuddered at the sight, and trembled all the more at the angry threats now thundered forth from the mouth of the Giant.

This was Saturday—the end of a weary week, four days of which had been already spent in the dark dungeon-keep. A new spirit now possesses the imprisoned Pilgrims—"they begin to pray." Their prayer was like the wrestling of Jacob; it continued all night, even

---
*John Newton, "Jesus My All."

to the break of day; and that new day was the Sabbath. Bunyan evidently desires to leave on record in his immortal Allegory some testimony in honor of the Lord's day, and of its blessed privileges. So, upon this day of rest, this day of peculiar prayer, he represents the dawn of deliverance beaming upon the prisoners of Despair, who now become "prisoners of Hope." And is it not true that the Sabbath-day, by its holy rest and hallowed ministrations of the Word and prayer, breaks many a fetter, frees many a slave, dissolves the doubts of the week past, and delivers many a soul from the bondage of Despair?

A key called Promise.—In prayer comes the realization of the promises. Every prayer is founded on a promise, and every true prayer discovers this foundation. The promises of God, all of which are "yea and amen in Christ Jesus," penetrate every gloom and look beyond the thickest darkness. The promises fringe the thunder-cloud with rays of light, and enable us to discern the "smiling face" behind the "frowning providence." Promise sees the dawn from the midnight, anticipates the sunrise from the sunset, recognizes in the leafless trees and cheerless snows of winter the harbinger and earnest of the fruits and flowers and seasonable enjoyments of the summer-tide. The Key of Promise now opens the doors and iron gates of the dungeon of Doubting Castle, and delivers the Pilgrims out of the hands of Giant DESPAIR. So they escaped, and once more return to the narrow way.

Bunyan's descriptions and delineations of the doubting character of Christians constitute some of the most striking and instructive portions of his writings. He had been himself much exercised and tried by doubts and fears, and even by despair; and in the school of experience he learned the great lesson he here teaches us. He therefore lays stress upon this feature of Christian experience. In his "Holy War" he describes a formidable force as having been sent against Mansoul, consisting of "an army of terrible *doubters*." The three great divisions of this army were (1) the election doubters; (2) the vocation doubters; and (3) the grace doubters. He further develops this great topic in the scene now before us.

CHAPTER XVI.

THE DELECTABLE MOUNTAINS.

INTRODUCTION.—The Pilgrims have now attained to an advanced stage of their journey, to that point of elevation, the distant prospect of which CHRISTIAN had been permitted to see from the Palace Beautiful, and of which the fair sisterhood of the palace had informed him, saying, "When thou comest there, from thence thou mayest see the gate of the Celestial City." Arrived at this point, CHRISTIAN and his comrade are introduced to the Shepherds who fed their Master's sheep, and with pastoral care tended the flocks committed to their charge. These are the Delectable Mountains; and the country is called IMMANUEL'S LAND. The Shepherds are the appointed pastors of the flock of God; and now for a season our Pilgrims are confided to their ministration, for instruction and advice.

This is accomplished in two ways—by a Retrospect, and by a Prospect. These Shepherds point out to the Pilgrims some of the dangers of the way, by the view from Mount Error, and (which still more nearly affected the past experience of the twain) the view from Mount Caution. They then proceed to the Prospect, as promised at the Palace Beautiful; and through the telescope they enable the Pilgrims, indistinctly, indeed, but yet in some appreciable measure, to behold the gates of the City.

Here the Pilgrims are represented as having risen from the low level of doubt and desperation to a very exalted platform of Christian privilege and opportunity. Under the instruction of the Shepherds, and from the lofty stand-point of their present experience, they view the fearful depths of woe from which they have been rescued, and thereby learn to magnify that sparing grace that hath redeemed them from destruction. They are also assisted to entertain clear views and bright prospects through the telescope of Faith; and are made to feel that they are "nearing sunrise," and are as citizens already arrived at the suburbs of their Home. "Now is your salvation nearer than when you believed!"

The Delectable Mountains.—Days of peace and a season of repose are granted to the Pilgrims after their hard experiences in Doubting Castle. A pastoral scene opens upon their view, and by-and-by they are in the midst of orchards, and vineyards, and flowing fountains, and refreshing fruits—indicative of the high privileges and seasonable comforts that refresh the souls of them that are weary.

Here are pasture-grounds and flocks of sheep, and shepherds tending them—a lovely illustration of "the Church of God, which he hath purchased with his own blood," Acts 20:28. Here are the under-shepherds, in charge of the folds of sheep, and responsible to "the Great Shepherd and Bishop (overseer) of our souls." Just such a scene as is described by the prophet in view of the Gospel-day—"How beautiful upon the mountains are the feet of him that bringeth good tidings, that publisheth peace; that bringeth good tidings of good, that publisheth salvation; that saith unto Zion, Thy God reigneth," Isaiah 52:7.

By the highway side.—These Shepherds watch for souls; and therefore do they stand in the thoroughfare, where pilgrims pass, and need their counsel and communion for the further stages of the journey. The names of the Shepherds are suggestive, embracing the main features of the true Christian minister. Rarely, indeed, are all these combined in any very high degree in any one person. The great lesson, however, is—not a fourfold classification of different gifts, but (as far as God's grace and human opportunity may permit) the combination of these fourfold gifts and graces in every minister of Jesus Christ.

KNOWLEDGE—Under the Jewish dispensation it was required that "the priest's lips should keep knowledge," Malachi 2:7. How much more must this be demanded of the Christian minister, whose office it is to instruct the people in the things of God; to feed the sheep and to tend the lambs of the flock!

EXPERIENCE—Knowledge for the head, experience for the heart—"for the perfecting of the saints, for the edifying of the body of Christ," Ephesians 4:12. This is the secret of an experimental ministry. He that draws water for himself from the wells of salvation, will be able most plentifully to supply the spiritual wants of others.

WATCHFUL—Knowledge may sleep, and experience may nod to slumber; but watchfulness tends to keep both awake, and to sustain both in action. The true minister is a Watchman, a wakeful sentinel—"all eye, all ear, all expectation of the coming foe." It is for him to keep the sheep, to guard the fold. Therefore says the Apostle—"They watch for your souls, as they that must give account."

SINCERE—Not gifts only, but graces also—graces to use well the gifts. SINCERE involves all that is included within the meaning of a *true* man; whose heart believes what his lips declare; whose breast is filled with the love of Christ and the love of souls. SINCERE is no hireling shepherd; in a sincere heart and fervently he loves the sheep, and guides them safely to the fold.

Some wonders.—The Pilgrims sleep, and are refreshed. They awake for spiritual communion with the Shepherds; and as they walk and talk together, they see "a pleasant prospect on every side." These are some of the blessed privileges of Immanuel's Land. But there are other views which must be pointed out ere they depart.

In the midst of privileges there are manifold dangers. Here, on the Delectable Mountains, is the Mount of Error. Over its lowering crest they look down its precipitous sides to its deep base beneath; and there they see the victims of Error in religion. Take heed, ye sheep, that ye wander not to this dangerous height! Take double heed, ye Shepherds—for yourselves and for the flock—lest ye be responsible for the downfall of some!

Another height is called Mount Caution. This is a point, not of danger, but of admonitory observation. The view hence is full of deep meaning, especially to our Pilgrims. A bold and masterly reminiscence is this, showing how far they had themselves already wandered; ay, and a little farther! There was the well-remembered "stile," and there its deceptive path through the meadow-land, and there its destination—Doubting Castle. All this the Pilgrims knew by sad, sad experience. But Divine mercy, and their realization of the promises, had delivered them; and now they are permitted to see what that deliverance involves. Here, on the Mountains Delectable, are the delivered captives looking down upon the captives that have never been set free—the blind victims of DESPAIR, dwelling among the tombs of dead men, blindly and vainly groping, where no light, or joy, or liberty, ever dawn again, and all is doubt and darkness and despair. Oh, how their view did magnify the greatness of that love that did deliver them from such a deep and dark captivity!

A by-way to hell.—How dreadful to contemplate, that in the fairest places of Christian privilege are found the greatest penalties of disobedience! Yes, this is the place where the "many stripes" are earned. There are some who go straight to hell, by the open and avowed path of ungodliness. There are others who walk in profession of religion, clad in the King's livery, using the Master's name, and who yet, through some by-way, shall be cast into outer darkness from the brilliantly lighted festive hall. "If therefore the light that is in thee be darkness, how great is that darkness!"

A high hill, called Clear.—Here is the fulfillment of the promise of the fair sisters of the Palace Beautiful—the promised prospect of the Celestial City. And now, amid the terrors of the Lord, the fair prospect opens in the distance. The dazzling glory of the view is tempered by the frame and feeling of their minds, thus toned to sad reflection by what they have just beheld.

And now, with trembling hand and with dimly-visioned eye they take the Telescope of Faith, and see, "as through a glass, darkly," the far-off gates of bliss—"they *thought* they saw something like the gate." This was a view "not clear, nor dark." The promise of the virgins of the Palace had been somewhat shaded by the Pilgrims' recent unbelief and departure from the way, and by their present realization of what might have been involved in that departure from the beaten track. The Telescope of Faith must not be darkened by unbelief, nor the prospect clouded by mists and vapors of doubt and fear. The clearness of the view from this spot is regulated by the same law as the depth of the fords of the River by-and-by—"as you *believe* in the King of the place."

What blessed views are opened up to the clear eye of Faith, where there are no doubts, no fears, no sins, to unnerve the hand, to dim the eye, to dull the glass, or to cloud the prospect!

> "My Father's house on high,
>   Home of my soul! how near,
> At times, to Faith's far-seeing eye,
>   Thy golden gates appear!"

With this scene, and the parting gifts of the Shepherds, a break occurs in the Allegory, "So I awoke from my dream," saith the Dreamer. Stay, he shall yet dream again! The end of the pilgrimage has only been revealed in prospect; but the Pilgrims are not yet "At home."

CHAPTER XVII.

THE ENCHANTED GROUND, AND THE DESCENT THERETO.

INTRODUCTION.—In the midst of blissful revelations, somewhat chequered by at least one dreadful scene of admonition, the Dreamer awakes. But by-and-by he dreams again. The same two Pilgrims are presented to his view; they have now reached the level plains, and have once more to meet the perils of the way. Here, fresh visions are vouchsafed, and new lessons taught.

By a "crooked lane," from the country of Conceit, IGNORANCE enters on the pilgrimage. Of him we shall learn more by-and-by. Meanwhile, a critical stage of the journey is being passed, with present evidences and by-gone reminiscences of danger. Here TURN-AWAY is stayed in his unworthy career, and, by his awful fate, fills up a portion of the picture of the Allegory. And here, too, is the place where LITTLE-FAITH was once overpowered by the assault of the robbers and bandits of the way, leaving an admonitory lesson, and a comforting truth withal, for those who would afterwards pass that way. "A little crooked lane," "a very dark lane," and "Deadman's lane," are here set forth as perilous places, for admonition; and "*Little*-faith" as the single ray of hope.

The conversation between the Pilgrims, on the Enchanted Ground, supplies what knowledge we have of HOPEFUL'S earlier experiences—his convictions, the struggles of his conscience, and his ultimate conversion. In this we shall find how it was that FAITHFUL sowed the good seed in the heart of HOPEFUL; and the martyr of Vanity Fair, "though dead, yet speaketh." It is an interesting study for thoughtful and spiritually-taught minds to trace the ordeal of HOPEFUL'S earlier stages of enlightenment, and how it was that he at last attained to a full and complete salvation in the revelation of Jesus to his spiritual apprehension. The workings of Divine grace in the soul, and the gradual progression of light and knowledge, are well set forth in this conversation, from the first dawn of conviction to the patient praying of that prayer—"Father!

reveal thy Son!" and the answer to the prayer, in the manifestation of the Lord's Christ to the eyes of his spiritual understanding.

The same two Pilgrims.—The preceding scene had broken the slumbers of the Dreamer; but he turns once more upon his side, and dreams again. It is not a new dream, but a continuance of the old. He sees the same twain Pilgrims. On his awaking, he had left them on the heights; on his sleeping again, he sees them in the hollows—pursuing the selfsame pilgrimage. The Dream does not lose sight of its great heroes; and God does not lose sight of his faithful children: "He which hath begun a good work in you, will perform it until the day of Jesus Christ," Philippians 1:6.

A little crooked lane.—Not by the "strait gate," but by the "crooked lane," has this new Pilgrim obtained admittance to the "Narrow-way," in his journey from the country of Conceit. Men that are wise in their own conceits consider their own way to be the best, and discern not the crookedness of the path they tread. Here is introduced a Pilgrim, who subsequently travels even to the gates of the Celestial City, and there meets his final destiny. A character that travels thus far, and approaches thus near to the end of the Progress, surely demands the serious attention of all. If we would "finish our course *with joy,*" we do well to take warning by the example of IGNORANCE.

A very dark lane.—This is evidently a perilous portion of the journey. Dangers are multiplied here, and the Pilgrims must needs be circumspect. This is the "dark lane" of perdition to at least one man, who is borne thence in the strong custody of devils. The remembrance of what the Shepherds had shown them is revived in the minds of our Pilgrims, by the fate of this victim of darkness, when they observed how he was cast into the door in the side of the Hill. And this remembrance awakens other reminiscences of the dangers of the place. Here, CHRISTIAN tells the story of one of the Pilgrims of former days—a story illustrative of some of the tests and trials of Faith, how nearly it may be overborne, and may at last be left, as it were, half-dead.

Little-faith.—The mention of this man's name introduces a very instructive episode of the narrative. The "many ways that butt down" upon the path are doubly dangerous—

(1) to the false Pilgrims who walk therein, and who enter the Narrow-way thereby and

(2) to the true Pilgrims who tarry near those devious paths.

Thieves and robbers enter by these side avenues, and by their assaults they ofttimes do injury to the Pilgrims of Sion.

This man, LITTLE-FAITH, not heeding the danger, had sat down at the junction of Deadman's lane with the Narrow-way. Here he was overpowered by the desire to slumber, and he slept. This was neither the time nor the place for sleep; hence the sequel—the assault by FAINT-HEART, MISTRUST, and GUILT.

This is a remarkable description of the dangers incident to *littleness* of Faith. There are degrees of Faith; some stronger, some weaker; some greater, some lesser; and according to its strength or weakness is the experience of its possessor. The man of little faith is more susceptible of alarms, more liable to assaults, and more vulnerable in the fight, than he that has great faith. Thus LITTLE-FAITH is exposed to three successive assaults, progressive in their character and consequences. Through the weakness of his faith, his heart is faint; he is brought to a standstill; he has no boldness or resolution; and his fears are more than his faith. This is straightway followed by a distrustful spirit, by which the Pilgrim loses many of the marks and tokens of his acceptance. And, having thus far suffered by these successive assaults, his faith becomes yet more feeble, and by-and-by he falls a victim to guilt, and is brought low, even to the dust of spiritual degradation, and to the poverty and need of spiritual loss. Whoso gives way to a *faint heart* in the pilgrimage, will soon *mistrust* the comforts and promises of God, and ere long this will amount to *guilt* of soul and conscience—and all through *littleness* of Faith!

Most of his spending money.—This was the amount of LITTLE-FAITH'S loss. The "pearl of great price" was his main capital; his comfort, and confidence, and assurance are the dividend or income, which will be more or less, in proportion as the value of the treasure of the heart is realized by faith. Over and above the jewels of the Kingdom are the joys and consolations of the Christian, that tend to mitigate the burden and heat of the day, and to shorten the weariness of the journey home. These are the incidental possessions of the Pilgrim; the circumstantials, but not the essentials, of his assurance and acceptance. Hence, Bunyan calls them "his spending money"—those minor joys, and passing sunshine, that may be clouded and darkened, that are liable to the ebb and flow of spiritual tides, and rise or fall according to the fluctuations of faith. Littleness of faith will have littleness of realization; and when it is faint-hearted, and exposed to the doubts and suspicions of mistrust, it forfeits confidence, suffers spiritual loss, and becomes otherwise impoverished.

They got not his jewels.—The main capital, the treasure of the heart, is safe. That treasure is in heaven, where thieves do not break through nor steal. His faith, though *little*, is *alive*. If it were great faith, it would reap great profits and enjoyments; but this man's faith is small, and therefore he realizes but little of the joys and consolations of the way. These "jewels" are the essentials of the man of God—living faith, holy love; the certificate of acceptance—"the witness of the Spirit," which is the credential of the pilgrimage. LITTLE-FAITH still possesses these; they are in safe custody—"hid with Christ in God." His gold, and his greater and more costly treasures, are entrusted, not to his own frail custody, but to a faithful Creator, to whom he has committed the keeping of his soul, (1 Peter 4:19). Thus does Bunyan further illustrate his meaning, when, in his "Grace Abounding," he says—"Oh, I saw that my gold was in my trunk at-home, in Christ my Lord and Savior. Now, Christ was all; all my wisdom, all my righteousness, all my sanctification, and all my redemption!"

The preservation of his "jewels" was owing to two reasons—(1) because they were treasured up in heaven; and (2) because they were held as of no account on earth.

(1) They were treasured up in heaven: The heavenly treasure is never committed to the sole charge and custody of human hands. The Christian Pilgrim's treasure is not here, but laid up in heaven. The road of life is far too dangerous for so great a charge as this. Therefore, like careful travelers, we journey lightly here; the heavy and material things are in the charge of One who can keep that which is committed to his trust. Thus the true Christian sits loose to the things of this world; his treasure is in heaven, and his heart is there also.

> "What have I left, that I should stay and groan?
>   The most of me to heaven has fled.
> My joys and hopes are all packed up and gone;
>   The rest must follow on with speed."

(2) They are held as of no account on earth: The pearl of great price is not an article of earthly exchange; nor is it to be had for any earthly cost. It is ignored here, as it was in Vanity Fair. Whoso would have it must search for it in heavenly fields, and dig for it as for hid pearls. "Without money and without price" is the condition of

the gift; and if sold for earthly dross, this would constitute no spiritual gain. Even a *little* faith is the "gift of God," held in safe trust for man by him who is the Giver of the gift.

The subsequent conversation between CHRISTIAN and HOPEFUL is aptly introduced at this point of the narrative; illustrative of the difficulty of the warfare, the formidable nature of the spiritual antagonists, and the little reliance to be reposed in our own strength. HOPEFUL'S observations evidently prove that he has never experienced the strife, and knows not what the character of the warfare is; whereas, CHRISTIAN speaks out of the fullness of his own experience, as a disciplined soldier of the Cross, who has suffered adversity, and met with sharp reverses, and through fields of blood fought on to victory.

The King's Champion.—This was GREAT-GRACE. He stands in contrast to LITTLE-FAITH. Both were subjects of the King, but (as Bunyan says), "all the King's subjects are not his champions." The strong are designed to help the weak. And yet, even GREAT-GRACE has need to be watchful. The scars on his face prove how real is the conflict sometimes; and that, with all the grace that is supplied to God's children, the best and bravest of them may be brought under the power of fear, faint-heartedness, and guilt.

Two things become us to do.—Seeing that such are the perils of the way, it behooves us that we take all due precaution ere we commit ourselves to the journey, and that we give all diligence, when, having begun, we proceed upon the pilgrimage.

1. The first counsel is, that we be harnessed for the way: Here, CHRISTIAN speaks from experience. How ill-prepared had he been for the assault of APOLLYON, had he not been armed in the Palace Beautiful! Even *with* his armor, he found the battle to be sore and long, and for a time uncertain.

2. That we desire of the King a convoy: Alone, we cannot safely walk; alone, we cannot fight and be victorious. We must seek the presence and providence of God to attend us in all the stages of our pilgrimage—"If thy presence go not with me, carry us not up hence!" In times of war, the precious craft and cargo are convoyed across the seas, and in dangerous journeys escorts are furnished to conduct the caravans of pilgrims. So in the Christian pilgrimage, all times and places are fraught with danger; and the provision of help is everywhere and always a wise precaution. This will be more clearly seen in the second part of the Progress, where GREAT-HEART escorts the second Pilgrimage to the journey's end.

They saw a way.—Another seeming parallel presents itself. But at this point the two roads seem to be so equally straight, as to cause the Pilgrims to "stand still to consider." It is plain that now they "lean to their own understanding;" for, instead of pausing to take counsel with each other, they ought to have consulted the map of the way which had been given them by the Shepherds. This they failed to do; and thus one of the great lessons of the past was despised or forgotten. So, in the moment of their perplexity, Satan appears, having transformed himself into the appearance of an angel of light.

> "Though he seem so bright and fair,
> Ere thou trust his proffered care,
> Pause a little, and beware!"*

They followed him.—This departure from the right way was not because of any desire to choose an easier path, nor for the avoidance of any hardship or difficulty, nor for any apparent superiority of one road above the other; but simply through the Pilgrims' forgetfulness of the counsel of the Shepherds. They were in doubt, and needed some one to advise them. The "note of the way" had been given them for the solution of such perplexities. Their sin was, not that they paused to consider, but that they omitted to consult the map. This "note of the way" is the Bible, in its higher and more spiritual direction to advanced pilgrims, who, by reason of their exercised experience, are exposed to the more subtle and spiritual temptations of the Evil One.

In this, the Pilgrims had, moreover, neglected the second kindly counsel of the Shepherds—"to beware of the flatterer." Thus they had committed two evils—in rejecting the counsel of God, and in accepting the counsel of Satan.

Accordingly, chastisement follows; yet not in judgment, but in mercy. God always grieves, with a true Father's tenderness, to see his children go astray; and, rather than give them over to their sin, he follows to reclaim them. This Shining One, with a whip of small cords, is the Fatherhood of God, dealing with his erring children. His chastisement is love. These stripes and scourges are not for his pleasure, but "for our profit, that we might be partakers of his holiness," Hebrews 12:10.

His name was Atheist.—This second danger was also foreseen by the Shepherds, and a timely caution given to beware. How different

---

*Adelaide Anne Procter, "A False Genius."

are the temptations of the way! One beguiles the Pilgrims into snares by flattering words; while another laughs to scorn the hope of the pilgrimage.

ATHEIST would fain laugh down the evidence of faith, because he has not *seen* the better land with his bodily eyes. His only argument is ridicule; his only evidence is sight. He believes no future harvests, because he *sees* not the golden sheaves in the seed-time. He receives not the bank-note, because he *sees* not the substance of its promise. But "faith is the substance of things hoped for, the evidence of things not seen," Hebrews 11:1.

And this faith—trusting, believing, farseeing faith—sustains the Pilgrims, "Did we not *see* from the Delectable Mountains the gate of the City?" Yes, with the quickened eye of Faith they had spiritually *seen* the land afar off. This is the privilege of God's own children. "Eye hath not seen, nor ear heard, neither have entered into the heart of man the things which God hath prepared;" therefore ATHEIST cannot see the end of the journey. "But God hath revealed them *unto us* by his Spirit;" therefore CHRISTIAN and HOPEFUL have seen the land and the good things which God hath prepared "for them that love him," (1 Corinthians 2:9–11).

This evidence of their faith cannot be overthrown—"Did we not *see* the gate of the City?" Thus true experimental faith can answer the objections of unbelievers. It is the inner testimony, the witness of the heart. This answer was not designed to convince ATHEIST, but to strengthen their own consistency, and to assist them to "beware of the flatterer." Such is the value of these blessed views revealed by faith: they communicate present joy, and inspire future confidence. One such vision of the otherwise Unseen is calculated to dispel a thousand doubts of unbelief. If it be not an answer to the world, it is a sufficient answer to one's own soul, sustaining the spirit of faith, and hope, and confidence in God. Oh, for such faith as Moses had! "for he endured, as seeing Him who is invisible."*

The Enchanted Ground.—The third caution of the Shepherds is now brought to mind—"to take heed that they slept not on the Enchanted Ground." The Pilgrims have now entered on that region of country, and they feel the spirit of slumber steal softly over them, and their eyes are heavy with sleep. CHRISTIAN exhorts his comrade to be wakeful and vigilant.

The Enchanted Ground means—politically—the mitigation of

---

*Hebrews 11:27—By faith he forsook Egypt, not fearing the wrath of the king: for he endured, as seeing him who is invisible.

penalties and persecutions; when ease and liberty are enjoyed, and the Church has rest from strife. This is a season fraught with danger; lest a spirit of soft and luxurious ease should take the place of former vigilance and watchfulness. Spiritually (and here is its real significance), the Enchanted Ground is meant to indicate such seasons of worldly prosperity as tend to render Christian men careless and "at ease in Sion." How often have men fallen from the consistency of the Christian walk, when visited with the sunshine of temporal success! "Give me not riches," said one of old, "lest I be full, and deny thee, and say, Who is the Lord?" Proverbs 30:8–9.

Such is the position of our Pilgrims at this stage of their journey. They are represented as tarrying for a time in a land of luxury and ease. They need to "watch and be sober." The whole tendency of such a season is in the direction of sloth, and slumber, and forgetfulness of God. To resist this temptation, they resort to the blessed expedient of Christian communion, and fellowship of saints. Soft indulgence tends to blunt the keen edge of Christian experience; but, in Christian communion, "iron sharpeneth iron." It is highly profitable to the soul's health to review the past, to remember the days of old, and to call to remembrance the way in which the Lord hath led us.

Where God began with us.—In this godly intercourse, we do well to begin, as the Pilgrims did, "where God began with us." This conversation conducts us through the past experiences of HOPEFUL—from his former darkness to his present enjoyment of light in the Lord.

HOPEFUL was once an inhabitant of Vanity Fair; in all respects conformed to the vanities of that sinful place. His observation of CHRISTIAN and FAITHFUL first led him on the way towards newness of life. He began, as most men begin, by strong conviction of his sin, and of his consequent danger. He however, sought to stifle these convictions, and to blind himself to the real peril of his state. He tells us what were the chief causes of this resistance to the strivings of the Spirit.

1. His ignorance of God's mode of operation.—He had never trod this path before, and his carnal heart would not admit that this was God's work in his soul. He thought not that God would accomplish the cleansing of his conscience by first stirring it to its depths, and revealing all its hidden defilement.

2. Sin was yet sweet to his taste.—Sin had struck its fibers deep into his soul, and had twined itself around the affections of his heart. Therefore he was loth to leave it. Alas! these fondled sins,

these idols of the heart—how they gather round us, and do so easily beset us, and hinder us in running the race that is set before us!

3. Unwillingness to part with old companions.—As are our sins, so are our partners in sin. Friendships are formed, and we are unwilling to abandon them; and the companionships being unchanged, the soul continues in the bond of iniquity. Such are the stern demands of righteousness, that sin must be plucked up, even to the last, the least, the lowest fiber of its root.

4. The seasons of conviction were sore and trying.—And therefore he sought to be rid of them, as one would be rid of unquiet hours, and days of anguish and sore affliction. Ah, what a coward is the conscience when brought face to face with its own sins, and forced to fight its fierce battle of conviction!

Such were the strivings of HOPEFUL'S conscience; at one time rampant, at another time restrained; rising to convulsive throes as circumstances provoked its sensitiveness. What a creature of circumstances is an awakened conscience! As Madame de Staël observes—"The voice of conscience is so delicate, that it is easy to stifle it; but it is also so clear that it is impossible to mistake it." The sight of a good man, the testimony of a verse of Scripture, an aching head, a trifling illness, a tolling bell, a passing funeral, a serious reflection, or a thought of death—any of these would suffice to revive the power of conscience in the awakened sinner.

HOPEFUL, thus pursued by an unquiet conscience, sought refuge in reformation of life. He left off doing evil, and applied himself to the performance of religious duties. This was a step in the right direction, but it was not everything. Sin must be dealt with, not only as to its outward fruits, but also as to its innermost root. If the fountain be not cleansed, the stream cannot be continuously clean. If the corrupt tree be not wholly healed at the root, nothing yet is done.

Bunyan introduces much of his own experience into this description of HOPEFUL'S spiritual state. In his "Grace Abounding" he tells of his own reformation of life—"Thus I continued about a year; all which time our neighbors did take me to be a very godly man, and did marvel much to see such a great and famous alteration in my life and manners; and, indeed, so it was, though yet I knew not Christ, nor grace, nor faith, nor hope."

Thus far had HOPEFUL attained; and yet he was not satisfied with his spiritual progress. Sin was not uprooted; sin entered into, and intermingled with, all his deeds. A better righteousness than his own must needs be provided, if his soul is to be fully and finally saved. Here he breaks his mind to FAITHFUL, and is by him instructed to seek "the righteousness of One who never had sinned."

The conversation now unfolds the great essential doctrine of the cross—the imputed righteousness of Jesus Christ, who had no sin, but was "made sin" for us, "that we might be made the righteousness of God in him," 2 Corinthians 5:21. HOPEFUL rejoices in this precious truth, and at once begins to seek, for this righteousness; so that of him it may now be said—"Behold, he prayeth!" And what earnest prayer, what wrestling agony was this! Undaunted by failure, again and again he prays, and at last receives the great revelation to his soul—"the Father showed me his Son!"

What effect this had.—Such a revelation of Jesus to the soul must surely have been confirmed by signs following. This view of Jesus was all-in-all to the anxious awakened sinner. It was the Wicket-gate, and the view of the Cross, and release from his burden, and pardon and peace—all in one. This was the secret of that "brotherly covenant," into which HOPEFUL had entered with CHRISTIAN, when proceeding forth from Vanity Fair as his companion to the Celestial City.

CHAPTER XVIII.

IGNORANCE.

INTRODUCTION.—The Pilgrims are still passing through the Enchanted Ground. They have thus far, in accordance with the advice of the Shepherds, resisted the spirit of slumber, by sustaining an interesting and instructive conversation on the matter of their spiritual experience. This vigilance of the Pilgrims is still further maintained by a spirited and suggestive argument with IGNORANCE, a man whom they have met on their descent from the Delectable Mountains. On their first meeting with him, as he entered by the "little crooked lane" from the country of Conceit, the Pilgrims had rebuked him for his self-righteousness and ignorance of the conditions of the Pilgrimage; they had then gone forward, leaving him for a time to muse upon their conversation.

CHRISTIAN AND HOPEFUL now invite this man once more to enter into companionship and intercourse. The report of their wayside interview occupies the following chapter; it opens up new views of the ignorance of the carnal heart, and presents some striking expositions of important truths, as delivered by our twain Pilgrims. There would seem to be a marked resemblance between IGNORANCE and a former Pilgrim, whose name was TALKATIVE. Both of these men possessed a certain amount of theoretic knowledge, but had no spiritual discernment to apprehend the truth aright. Both were vain boasters, self-saving, and self-righteous men. The ultimate fate of TALKATIVE is not recorded: but the career of IGNORANCE is traced to the end of the pilgrimage, to the very threshold of the Celestial City. With the awful end of this ignorant professor of religion the curtain falls and the Allegory concludes. But we will not anticipate the narrative, and would now call attention to the following instructive conversation.

Saw Ignorance coming after.—This man had been allowed time and opportunity to ponder in his heart the things already spoken by the Pilgrims. He is, however, a stranger to such teaching, and savoreth not the conversation or companionship of such men. He therefore "loitereth behind," seeking rather to avoid their company, and, in his self-sufficiency, to walk alone. Elements that are unlike do not easily intermingle. When Jesus came as the Light into this dark world, it is said—"The light shineth in darkness; and the darkness comprehended it not," John 1:5; and again, "Every one that doeth evil hateth the light, neither cometh to the light, lest his deeds should be reproved," John 3:20.

Let us talk away the time.—Still to resist the spirit of slumber, is the duty of the Pilgrims, at least until they have got quite over the Enchanted Ground. Another opportunity is thus created in the Allegory for the introduction of doctrinal truth in contrast to the misapprehensions of spiritual ignorance.

So they begin to question with IGNORANCE, and thus they draw him out in conversation. The self-satisfaction of this man is evident from the very outset. "To think of God and heaven" he deems to be the sum and substance of religion; and to "desire" the possession of God and heaven, he esteems as a distinguishing characteristic of his spiritual state. Poor IGNORANCE knows not that the very devils "think" much of God, and that even the worst of sinners do "desire" the things of heaven.

His own "heart" is the witness that lays the flattering unction to this man's soul. But the heart is "deceitful," and cannot be trusted; and, besides, it is not an independent witness, but mere self-testimony. It needs the witness of the Spirit, and the witness of the Word, to tell the true testimony respecting our hearts, and to say "how it stands between God and our souls."

Good thoughts respecting ourselves.—The best thoughts we can entertain respecting ourselves are, that we have no good thing dwelling in us by nature; that the whole heart and life are corrupt and evil; that our spiritual health is diseased; and that we need a Physician, a Helper, a complete Savior; and that without this salvation, we are lost, and lost forever. These are the thoughts that spring from "heart-humiliation," and consciousness of sin.

The self-righteous spirit of the unregenerate man arises from many secret sources, deeply laid in the carnal and unrenewed heart:

(1) from an *over-estimation* of self—"the righteousness of the Scribes and Pharisees;"

(2) from an *under-estimation* of what God requires of us—a perfect righteousness;

(3) from *ignorance* of self—"thinking ourselves to be something, when we are nothing;" and

(4) from *forgetfulness* of our actual condition—forgetting ourselves as we really are. In the mirror of God's Word, and in the light of his Holy Spirit, we are permitted to behold ourselves as in a glass, and thus to dispel self-ignorance (James 1:25).

Good thoughts concerning God.—All men think some thoughts respecting God; and their thoughts are generally "good thoughts," that is, they think good of him, because God is good, and he is the Author and Giver of all good things. It is also possible to entertain good thoughts of God, theologically, as to his attributes—his love, and power, and such like. But these thoughts do not necessarily make us to be good, much less do they constitute a state of salvation. What we need is, to realize our thoughts of God, and to apply them experimentally to ourselves. There are many who think of God as the Omniscient One, and yet, so little do they realize this thought, that they sin openly before his face and in his searching sight, as though he saw them not. Our good thoughts concerning God, to be of any use, must lead to those practical duties which we owe to God and to ourselves.

"I believe in Christ."—It is easy to *say* this, as in a creed or confession of faith. But this is not "believing in Christ." IGNORANCE could say this creed, and did say it, and, possibly, believed it too; and yet he was far from the possession and enjoyment of saving faith in Jesus. He believed with *historical* faith—that Christ was born, and lived, and died. He believed with *theological* faith—that in Christ is the justification of the sinner. And yet this man had no due appreciation of Christ's real character and work, or of its bearing upon his own salvation. Hence, the faith of IGNORANCE is proved to be a fantastical, false, presumptuous, and deceptive faith.

It is *fantastical faith*, being the mere creation of his own fancy, a misapprehension of the true nature of faith, and in no respect warranted by any authority of God's Word.

It is *false* faith. Justification is not the laying of Christ's righteousness *over* our filthy rags, to hide, or even to repair our own righteousness; but the exchange of our filthy rags *for* the robe of the Savior's righteousness. He "took *our sins*" and now invites us—"Take *my yoke* upon you."

It is *presumptuous* faith. Seeing that in the long run it tendeth to justify men's works, and their persons for their works' sake. It is not that our deeds are made holy through Christ, but that Christ's perfect work is imputed to us, for Christ's own sake. He had no sin *in* him, but our sin was laid *upon* him and therefore Jesus died for us. We have no righteousness *in* us, but his righteousness is laid *upon* us; and therefore we live in him.

It is *deceptive* faith. Having falsely conceived the nature of true faith, IGNORANCE has trusted, as it were, in the staff of a broken reed, whereon if a man lean, it will go into his hand and pierce it. Such trust, partly resting upon our own deeds, and partly upon the work of Christ, is dishonoring to Christ, to whom the whole work of salvation belongeth, from first to last; for Jesus is both "the author and the finisher of our faith." This true faith puts forth its hand, and takes the righteous robe: it is that faith "under the skirt of which, the soul being shrouded, and by it being presented as spotless before God, it is accepted."

If he had Christ revealed to him?—This question of HOPEFUL takes the direction of his own experience. In the preceding conversation between the Pilgrims, we have been informed how it was that HOPEFUL'S conversion was brought about, even as was the conversion of Paul—"It pleased God to reveal his Son in me," Galatians 1:15–16. But this experience is too deep, too lofty, too profound, too heavenly for IGNORANCE to comprehend or understand.

You go so fast.—Yes, HOPEFUL has already proceeded in his spiritual teaching far beyond the power of IGNORANCE to follow. High as the heaven is the exalted doctrine of this devoted believer in Jesus, who has in his own experience "seen the Lord," in the spiritual vision of his soul. Behind such advanced Pilgrims, yea, very far behind, must such carnally-minded men as IGNORANCE walk.

True or right fear.—The reckless unconcern of IGNORANCE suggests to the pious mind of HOPEFUL how good it would be for men's spiritual interests, if they were more actuated by the "fear" of God. CHRISTIAN would qualify the expression, and calls it "true or right fear," which is discovered by the following marks and tokens:—

1. By conviction of sin. This is the awakening of the soul, as from a deep slumber of ignorance and unconcern. It is the opening of the eyes to impending danger; the sensitiveness of the soul, enabling the sinner to *feel* the burden of his sin. Here, all as yet is fear and trembling, as CHRISTIAN himself once wept and trembled in the plain, and "brake out with a lamentable cry, saying, 'What shall I do?'" How can a man see himself in the midst of wrath, and not fear? How can he behold the mouth of hell, and not fear? How can he feel his weight of woe and condemnation, and not be affected

with fear? Such fear as this is that "true or right fear" that is akin to "godly sorrow," which "worketh repentance to salvation." (2 Corinthians 7:10).

2. By laying fast hold on the Savior. Consciousness of danger impels a man to seek for safety. Instant, earnest, and immediate is the effort of the shipwrecked mariner to strike out for the rock, and be safe. Who could stay the impetuous course of the man-slayer when pursued, so fast and so very near, by the avenger of blood? And Christ is our Refuge, the Rock of our strength, the God of our salvation. It is true, his love must draw us, and his compassion win us; but there is ground for fear, too, as an element of safety—fear of danger, that makes us flee from wrath, and take refuge in the arms of Jesus, "till this tyranny be over-past."

3. By the effect of pardon on the soul. "There is forgiveness with thee, that thou mayest be *feared,*" Psalm 130:4. God's forgiveness leads to fear; and why? An eloquent writer asks—"What is that strange and potent element in Divine forgiveness which makes the forgiven fear—making me more afraid to sin beside the Cross of Calvary, with its quiet, pale, dead, bleeding burden, than if I stood at the foot of Sinai amid the thunders, lightnings, and trumpet peals that made Moses himself exceedingly fear and quake?"

The pardoned sinner "fears" God, because he now is able to understand the enormity of his sin in the greatness of the ransom. If our sin were easily pardoned, we might lightly sin, and reckon again upon the round of easy pardon. But no; the pardon of the sinner has cost a price too awful to contemplate, has required a life too vast to estimate, and demanded a ransom in the person—the Divinely human person—of Jesus Christ, the Son of God; and this must not be trifled with.

"Did you know one Temporary?"—This is a backslider—one who received the Word, the good seed, but received it in thorny ground; and although the seed gave some promise of development, yet the prickly thorns did ere long arise and choke the seed, which having "no deepness of earth," soon withered away.

This evil influence was brought about by one SAVE-SELF. Here, in another form, is the spirit of self-sufficiency that seems to require no Savior, and to stand in need of no salvation. Alas! that Pilgrims should thus easily be persuaded to turn back! "Because they had *no root*, they withered away."

Thus begins the downward course of backsliders—They draw off their minds from things Divine. They then withdraw themselves from the private duties of religion. By-and-by they forsake the communion of saints. Ere long, they become captious and cynical. Now the tide turns in the fullness of its might, and these men resign themselves to positive iniquity and evil companionships. And now, having ventured thus far, they are borne into the adverse current, and are hurried away into the vortex; and ("unless," as Bunyan says, "a miracle of grace prevent it") they are, as IGNORANCE by-and-by will be, cast into the abyss of eternal wrath.

CHAPTER XIX.

THE LAND OF BEULAH—
THE FORDS OF THE RIVER—AT-HOME.

"Methinks I feel the balmy air
    Breathe on a pleasant land
'Mid joys so great and scenes so fair,
    In Beulah's plains I stand.
A land of everlasting spring,
    Of seasons bright and gay
Where birds are ever on the wing,
    And night is lost in day.

The turtle sings the whole day long,
    The birds in chorus sing
Their matin-hymn and even-song,
    To God, their God and King.
From gloom, and doubt, and dark despair,
    An endless rest is given;
The shining ones are walking there,
    The border-land of heaven!"

INTRODUCTION.—The Enchanted Ground has been passed in safety; the Pilgrims are now in the Land of Beulah. Peace! it is a marriage scene! far from APOLLYON'S wrath, far from the darkness of Death's shadow, far from even the sight of Doubting Castle—away upon the heights, embowered in vineyards and orchards of the choicest fruits, is the Land of Beulah.

Bright and blissful are the visions of their sleep, as now, released from the toil and travail of the way, they rest upon their peaceful pillow. "They are come unto Mount Sion and unto the City of the Living God, the heavenly Jerusalem." Yet, one step more; one more ordeal must be passed. A flowing River, dark and deep, touches the base of the mount, and divides things present from things to come. This River must be forded, and it is only buoyant Faith that can overpass it safely.

The "Glorious Dreamer" dreams great visions now—of earnest hope, and struggling faith, and dying fears, and death-bed consolations, and promises all blooming into full fruition, and the last conflict with the last enemy, and heaven's bright seraphs helping in the fight, and the final triumph, when, as men for ever free, the Pilgrims leap upon the heavenly shore! And there are shining ones in waiting, to conduct them to the gates of bliss; and after these, a company of the heavenly host arrive, the escort of their triumph, with trumpeters and heralds, greeting them with ten thousand welcomes. And now, heaven's gates lift up their heads, and the once Pilgrims enter into the presence of their Lord, and straightway are transfigured before Him—wearing crowns of shining gold, and clad in robes of everlasting light. The Progress is ended; the Pilgrims are at rest!

The Country of Beulah.—"Thou shalt no more be termed Forsaken; neither shall thy land any more be termed Desolate: but thou shalt be called Beulah: for the Lord delighteth in thee, and thy land shall be married," (Isaiah 62:4). Beulah means "MARRIED"; and, in prophetic language, it speaks of the final blessedness of the Church—the bride of Christ, when the Bridegroom shall return to his now widowed spouse, and the marriage contract shall be renewed. Here, the allusion is appropriated to the advanced stage of the Christian pilgrimage, which conducts the Pilgrims into the very suburbs of the land, and nigh unto the gates of the Celestial City.

"Let me die the death of the righteous!" Here is a description of a Christian's sun-setting in this world, and the rising gloriously in the other and the better land. Here is the peaceful quietude of the departing Christian, finishing his course with joy. Already does the communion of the skies commence; heavenly messengers, with messages of love and peace, hover round the bed of the Pilgrims. The storms of the pilgrimage are hushed to silence; fierce tempests cease to blow; all here is blessed sunshine calm and sweet repose—here in the Land of Beulah.

Nearer and nearer! It is a Progress still, and as yet they are not at home. The light now dazzles them with its exceeding glory; and they can yet behold it only "as through a glass, darkly;" but they are advancing "nearer and nearer." They have, however, two difficulties more to meet with, (1) the intervening river; and (2) that river must be crossed.

A river.—This is the River of Death; a river without a bridge to span it, and its waters are very deep. The men shuddered at the sight. Yes, Death is the "king of terrors" still! The requirement is sternly exacted—*"you must go through,* or you cannot come at the

THE LAND OF BEULAH.

gate." Yet, to believing faith is given a great reward—"you shall find it deeper or shallower, as you *believe* in the King of the place."

The Pilgrims would avoid the crossing of this river, if they could. It is a cold flood; a stormy sea; at best it is a bitter pang, the residue of the curse of sin. Even STAND-FAST, a brave and good comrade of the Second Pilgrimage, did with a shudder say, as he adventured himself into the flood, "The waters, indeed, are to the palate bitter, and to the stomach cold."

In these fords of the river are described two Christian deathbeds: the one filled with fears and terrors, his faith feeble and faint, and therefore the waters in proportion deep; the other, ever hopeful and still rejoicing, upholds his more feeble brother; and is himself upheld; his faith is firm, and therefore his footing is sure—"Be of good cheer, my brother; I feel the bottom, and it is good!" How long shall CHRISTIAN be thus pursued by the great enemy of souls? Would Satan have him even yet, and in death destroy him who in life had proved so faithful? Yea, even in the fords of the river Satan standeth at his right hand; as Bunyan elsewhere says—"I find he is much for assaulting the soul when it begins to approach towards the grave."

CHRISTIAN seems to have failed to gain the foot-hold of the promises in these deep waters. HOPEFUL feels that goodly ground-work, and would share this platform of his faith and confidence with his comrade, if he could. This hopeful companion suggests the promises of God, beckons his partner on in hope, points to the shining ones that wait to receive them on the further shore; but CHRISTIAN, by reason of his doubts and fears, cannot realize so bright a prospect of the coming end. And yet it is one of the precious promises that at last sustains him—"When thou passest through the waters, I will be with thee; and through the rivers, they shall not overflow thee;"* and boldly resting himself on the strength of this plighted word of his God and Father, the scales of darkness fall from his eyes, his feet are grounded on a sure place; and, ere long, both CHRISTIAN and HOPEFUL have gained the Eternal shore.

> "The world recedes, it disappears;
> Heaven opens on mine eyes; my ears
>   With sounds seraphic ring.
> Lend, lend your wings; I mount, I fly;

---

*Isaiah 43:2—When thou passest through the waters, I will be with thee; and through the rivers, they shall not overflow thee: when thou walkest through the fire, thou shalt not be burned; neither shall the flame kindle upon thee.

> O grave, where is thy victory?
> O death, where is thy sting?"*

Thus they went along.—The River of Death has been safely over passed. All that was mortal has been left behind; they now are disembodied spirits, unclothed of their mortality, and "clothed upon with their house which is from heaven," rising and soaring higher than the clouds. There, citizens of heaven receive them; ministering spirits, that once invisibly ministered to them here, now minister to them in glory, and open up the prospect of the things that yet shall be, and the part the redeemed shall yet bear in the coming kingdom of our Lord and of his Christ. Meanwhile the retinue enlarges, and swells into a glorious train of triumph and rejoicing; and, amid praises, and hallelujahs, and glad anthems of the skies, "an entrance is ministered unto them abundantly into the everlasting kingdom of our Lord and Savior Jesus Christ," 2 Peter 1:11.

Went in at the gate.—They have ascended the hill of the Lord; and now they enter by those golden gates, the object of their longing hope and expectations, for which they have been striving all their journey through. These are the Gates they had seen in the distance, through the telescope of faith. Their faith is now lost in sight; and there hope resigns her office, for all is full fruition. This is their Mount of Transfiguration—they shine resplendent as the sun when he shineth in his strength, with transformed powers to bear their transfigured glory.

I looked in after them.—As it were a glimpse, and but for a moment, revealed to the Dreamer; enough to tell him that heaven is more glorious than human words can possibly describe, or human heart conceive. As those great golden Gates turned for a brief moment on their hinges, a view is given along the golden streets— the grand and glorious vistas of the City of the Lord. And then the inner scene is closed to mortal eyes. The Pilgrims have reached their journey's end, and are safely housed in heaven. He that once wept and trembled outside the City of Destruction, now sings his salvation song within the walls of the heavenly Jerusalem—at home, at rest, for ever with the Lord!

> "His soul to Him who gave it rose;
> God led it to its long repose,
> Its glorious rest!
> And, though the warrior's sun has set,

---

*Alexander Pope, "The Dying Christian to His Soul."

> Its light shall linger round us yet,
> Bright, radiant, blest!"*

I wished myself among them.—Oh, that such blissful dreams could but become realities! Truly, one longs to be there, among the myriad choir, among the harpers harping upon their harps; to enter those pearly gates, to tread those golden streets, to wear those jeweled crowns, to wave those triumphant palms, and to be present with the Living Lord! But it must be to us, as it was to the Pilgrims—a PROGRESS; and if we patiently endure, as they did, to the end, we too shall be saved, and shall join them in the blessed throng of glorified saints in heaven.

Now, while I was gazing.—To please the taste, and to satisfy the utmost cravings of curiosity, Bunyan might well have concluded here. His Pilgrims once safe in heaven, what more can we need to know? But he writes his inimitable Dream, not only to please, but also to profit; not only to gratify, but also to admonish. And, accordingly, the finishing touch, with which he concludes his Allegory, is one of the darkest tints contained within the canvas of the picture. Scarce has he ceased to look upon the glories opened to his vision, his eyes yet dazzled by the sight, when he beholds just one more earthly scene, and with a shudder of alarm, the Dreamer awakes! What was this scene of horror?

As soon as the Dreamer had seen the last of the heavenly vision, he saw IGNORANCE come to the river-bank; and, strange to say, he crossed, without any difficulty, to the other side! This is a representation of the death of the self-righteous man. One VAIN-HOPE, a ferry-man, conducted him across the stream. What a masterly touch is this, descriptive of the death of thousands, who have no bands in their death, nor fear, as other folk! It is, perhaps, the only account we can give of the unconcern with which so many approach the realities of the death-bed; and if VAIN-HOPE be the ferry-man, Self-Righteousness is the ferry-boat. Ay, and large convoys of these spiritual emigrants are day by day being conveyed across in this frail, perilous bark, all-unconscious of the fathomless depths beneath, and of the vast future beyond.

IGNORANCE has crossed the flood of Death—all, both bad and good, must cross it somehow; but he meets no shining ones, and has no escort to the gates of the city. He has no credential, no pledge or token of acceptance, no sealed roll, no robe of righteousness, no

---

*Henry Wadsworth Longfellow, trans., "Coplas de Manrique."

wedding garment. So he answered never a word! Volubly enough did he talk to the Pilgrims in the Enchanted Ground; but now he has not a word to utter—he is "speechless," Matthew 22:12.

Here mark the difference!—The shining ones that had conducted CHRISTIAN and HOPEFUL to the Gates, are now commissioned to conduct IGNORANCE, bound hand and foot, to the Door in the side of the hill. The same angels that bind the wheat in sheaves, to be treasured in the garner, shall bind the tares in bundles, to be cast into the fire! And these shining ones executed the commission of their Lord. "Then I saw," says the Dreamer, "there was a way to hell, even from the gates of heaven, as well as from the City of Destruction!"

Thus, in this wondrous Allegory, the sinner is the last remembered, and his fate supplies the final touch; and with, the echoes of that awful sentence, still vibrating in the ears of Christendom, the First Part of the Dream concludes.

"So I awoke, and behold it was a Dream!"

" 'Twas not a vision of my sleep, nor dream that fancy paints;
It was a view of heaven itself, the dwelling-place of saints,
It was the glory of the Lord, the Spirit hath reveal'd,
The final happiness of those that God the Father seal'd.
This was the sight from which I woke, and looked and looked again,
And though their pilgrimage was o'er, I yet was on the plain;
And in the rugged wilderness, I looked and sighed in prayer,
'O God! complete my pilgrimage, conduct me safely there!' "

PART II.
CHAPTER I.

CHRISTIANA.

INTRODUCTION.—So CHRISTIAN completed his pilgrimage, and finished his course with joy. As a brave hero in the spiritual strife, we have followed his bold career. His like-minded companions, full of faith and hope, have well fulfilled their parts, and contributed not a little to the sustained interest of the story; yet, in the account of CHRISTIAN'S pilgrimage, we cannot forget that he has been alone, the one solitary member of his family who has adventured this great enterprise. He started alone, and trod the path of the highway alone, and alone he attained the goal of the pilgrimage—that is, without wife or child to cheer his chequered course, to support his oft-declining strength, or to bear him company in either his sorrows or his joys. And, for aught we know, the opposition offered by his family to his first setting out from the City of Destruction may have been continued even to his journey's end.

But, as often happens, that which a consistent life of faith cannot accomplish, a happy and triumphant death achieves. That stroke which smites so heavily upon the sympathies of the heart, and rends its fond affections, sometimes opens up the spring of living waters that has long been restrained within it, like a fountain within a rock. It is true of families, as it is of nations—"When thy judgments are in the earth, the inhabitants of the world will learn righteousness," Isaiah 26:9. This family circle had stood by the father's death-bed; were witnesses of his peace and joy, while for a space he spiritually tarried in the land of Beulah; had seen his struggle and his conflict with the last enemy, in the fords of the river; and observed how his anxious countenance at last beamed with a smile of triumphant joy, in the light of the precious promise of his God—"When thou passest through the waters, I will be with thee!" The rays of that sunset beckoned his wife and children after him; and to this we are indebted for the graphic account of the Second Pilgrimage.

I dreamed again.—The First Part of the PILGRIM'S PROGRESS had been written in the gaol of Bedford. The Second Part was produced a few years later, when, it would appear, Bunyan was again a free man, and residing in his native village of Elstow, which is "about a mile off the place" in which the former Part had been indited.

The second Dream is in many respects unlike its predecessor. The First Part is grave and weighty, stern and rugged in its experiences; the Second Part is of a more domestic and familiar character, entering into the ordinary associations of life, and dealing with family scenes and concerns of everyday experience. In the former Part we see great stalwart heroes of the Lord, who fill the canvas, and command the attention of the reader, like Elijah, or St. Paul. In this Second Part we come down to the level of domestic life, and are enabled to trace out the career of godly women and Christian children in the Pilgrimage of Sion.

It is the City of Destruction.—The story starts from the same point as before—the same City of Destruction, as populous, as profane, and as wicked as it had been in CHRISTIAN'S days. The by-gone pilgrimage, however, had come to be known and read of all men, and its protest against the wicked ways of the city left an impression upon the people's minds that could not easily be removed. The death of CHRISTIAN, answering so consistently to his holy life, had deepened this impression, and had inclined some of his former townsmen to follow his steps.

All our country rings of him.—This was true even in Bunyan's own day; how much more so now, when it may be said of all lands in Christendom—"There are but few houses that have heard of him and his doings, but have sought after and got the records of his pilgrimage." No book of uninspired origin has been more widely read than the PILGRIM'S PROGRESS.

Anything of his wife and children?—This question introduces the details of the Second Pilgrimage: CHRISTIANA had resisted conviction during the whole period of her husband's life-time. His death—when he had gone "over the river"—awakened her conscience to a sense of her own sin, and of her guilt in joining hand-in-hand with the ungodly, to resist good CHRISTIAN'S desires for heaven, and his earnest efforts to attain it.

Christiana had a dream.—She had three dreams—two for her admonition, and one for her encouragement. These dreams indicate the promptings of her mind, as they arose from the power of Satan, or from the struggles of Divine grace, or from the love of God revealing itself to her soul.

1. The dream of the broad parchment—the scroll of remembrance. This was for conviction of her sin. CHRISTIAN had felt his sin as the weary burden on his back, and CHRISTIANA now sees her sin unfolded to her conscience in the record of the roll. Thus, by different ways, conviction and consciousness of sin are brought home to the heart of the sinner.

2. The sight of the two ill-favored ones. This was an effort of the carnal mind to shake off conviction of sin, and to win back the awakened conscience to its sleep again. This dream was, however, in mercy suggested, being a presentiment of a scene by-and-by to happen; and a premonition to CHRISTIANA, who was thereby forewarned of a temptation that would ere long arise.

3. The vision of her husband in glory. This dream was sent for her encouragement. She is enabled in some measure to realize her husband's bliss, the glory that is beyond the tomb. She is thus encouraged to adventure the journey, for the attainment of "the rest that remaineth for the people of God."

One knocked hard at the door.—The inward musings of the awakened soul are answered by the outward calls of God's grace and the visits of his mercy. One now stands at the door, and knocks. His name is SECRET, from which we would gather that this messenger was a Divine person (see Judges 13:18, and marginal reading, compared with Isaiah 9:6). Here is Divine grace with a Divine hand knocking at the door of the widow's heart,

> "Soul, from thy casement look, and thou shalt see
> How He persists to knock and wait for thee!"*

SECRET, being in possession of God's mind, tells what is already known in heaven respecting CHRISTIANA'S spiritual state; and he comes with such kindly greetings and welcome invitations, as must have brought rich and abiding comfort and consolation to the oppressed spirit of the penitent. Oh, how blest are these tidings of pardon! these full and free promises of mercy! Is not this "good news" indeed, sweeter than honey to our taste, and soft as refreshing showers when they fall upon the parched and thirsty ground?

This Divine ambassador furthermore presents to CHRISTIANA the "golden letter" of the King. The golden counsel of this letter was— On to thy pilgrimage! tread the ground that CHRISTIAN trod; enter by

---

*Henry Wadsworth Longfellow, trans., "Tomorrow."

the Gate as CHRISTIAN entered; walk by the same rule; mind the same thing; sing these songs to cheer thee as thou goest; keep this counsel in thy bosom; and present it at the far gate! "The bitter is before the sweet."

The far gate.—There is a near gate—the "strait gate;" and there is a "far gate"—away in the distance; so narrow, that only true men can enter there, and yet so wide as to administer an "abundant entrance" to all God's children. Between the near gate and the far gate intervenes the path of the pilgrimage—"from this world to that which is to come."

Two of Christiana's neighbors.—Such holy determinations are not undertaken without strong opposition from the world and the things of the world. As CHRISTIAN had to resist the entreaties of his wife and neighbors, so CHRISTIANA must now be strong to resist the ill advice of those who would turn her feet back, ere she has well gained the threshold of the way. When God, by his awakening Spirit, knocks at the door of our hearts, we may be sure we shall hear other knocks besides—of those who would inquire what we mean to do, and whither we would go. One of these neighbors of CHRISTIANA strongly urges her to abandon her projected pilgrimage. Her name is Mrs. TIMOROUS. She has come of no worthy pedigree; her family failing being to turn people back from good designs and from heavenly intentions.

In vain does CHRISTIANA plead the inward convictions of the soul, which will not be set at rest by any other means; in vain does she plead the willingness of her children to accompany her; in vain does she relate her dreams, and the visit of the Man of God—TIMOROUS calls it "madness," and recites the difficulties and hardships of CHRISTIAN'S own experience, and, plausibly enough, reminds her that *he* was a strong man, but *she* a weak woman. Thus the tempters of this world do the duty of the great Tempter, and would dissuade even the true Pilgrims from their progress heavenward.

Tempt me not.—CHRISTIANA'S convictions were more to her than the plausible dissuasives of her neighbor. She therefore appeals to her that she cast no more temptation in her way, hindering her progress to the Kingdom, and prejudicing her fair prospects of future glory. "The bitter before the sweet!" Yes, the thorns first, and then the blooming rose; the rude, rough ploughshare first, and afterwards the golden harvests; the Cross, with all its weight and bitterness, and then the Crown!

"Come, neighbor Mercy."—The second of these two neighbors, it now appears, was one named MERCY. This is the introduction of one of the main characters of the Second Pilgrimage, who by-and-by joins herself to CHRISTIANA, and bears her company to the end. She had come, in questionable companionship, to remonstrate, but she remains to sympathize. Two causes contributed to this change of mind—

(1) Her sympathy for CHRISTIANA. The knowledge of another's sorrow and affliction ofttimes changes a spirit of reproof into a spirit of compassion. There is vast power in Christian earnestness, and much moral force in that deep-rooted solicitude, arising from heartfelt conviction of sin, which disposes the sinner to forsake all for Christ. This woman could not but feel that there was genuine reality in that self-denial, that now enables her neighbor to leave all and follow Jesus.

(2) Her anxiety respecting herself. This feeling, though not expressed at the time, yet abided deep in the heart of MERCY. She must look to herself, and see and judge whether these things are so, as reported by CHRISTIANA. Self-preservation is said to be the first law of nature; and so, in spiritual things, self-preservation may be said to be the first law of grace. MERCY decides to go with CHRISTIANA, and Mrs. TIMOROUS departs upon her way alone. Thus are fresh converts drawn to the cause of Jesus, and the world and Satan spoiled of some of their former subjects.

PART II.
CHAPTER II.

THE WICKET-GATE.

INTRODUCTION.—The Second Pilgrimage is begun; and more auspiciously, perhaps, than the First. A large group of Pilgrims—all of one household and family, now start for Sion, attended by a fair companion, whose name is MERCY. This group is gradually increased, by the addition of new comrades from time to time; and the whole company, in a diversified but yet consistent journey, march on to the better land.

We have set before us, in this Allegory, a beautiful illustration of Christian *female* character. In the former Part we have read the spiritual life of Christian men; but in this narrative it is Christian womanhood that is honored, in the representation of motherly influence, and sisterly companionship, and female piety, and filial following, and all the circumstances that go to make up the character of domestic Christian discipline, tempered by the spirit of home religion. The characters of CHRISTIANA and MERCY worthily occupy the foreground all through the Second Allegory, as those of CHRISTIAN and his comrades, FAITHFUL and HOPEFUL, in the First. Here we may see the Christian matron, and the Christian maid, and Christian children, all traveling the same pilgrimage, and helping each other forward in the heavenly race.

The setting out of CHRISTIANA, accompanied by MERCY, suggests a thought or two as to the respective reasons that urged them to undertake their pilgrimage.

CHRISTIANA is impressed with the fact that she has been directly *called* of God to commit herself to the way of holiness. Thus she interprets her dreams and visions, and, above all, the tidings that SECRET had told her, and the invitation he had borne for her acceptance from the King of the heavenly country. And in the firm persuasion of this call of God's own grace and love, she determines to forsake the City of Destruction, and to seek the heavenly rest, which, she is assured, is even now enjoyed by CHRISTIAN. In the strength and assurance of the heavenly calling, and with true earnestness of purpose, she betakes herself to her important enterprise.

MERCY accompanies her, not because of any known call of God, but (as she thinks) only on the invitation of CHRISTIANA. The maiden does not yet feel the movings and promptings of the Spirit (so as to know that they are of God), but has been attracted by the earnest spirit of her friend, besides being, in some measure, anxious about the safety of her own soul.

Thus it is that souls are brought to Christ—some directly, and others indirectly. Some are called sovereignly, by the voice of Jesus; while others are called instrumentally, by the service of godly men. Christ will have coworkers—"workers together with Christ Jesus." Paul came at the direct call of heaven; and the Gentiles came at the preaching of Paul. The woman of Samaria believed for the word of Jesus, and then proceeded to call her townsmen to the Messiah. And so, CHRISTIANA has been directly called by the invitation of the Savior, and MERCY follows in her train, bidden to the pilgrimage by the voice of our new Pilgrim. "How shall they hear without a preacher: and how shall he preach except he be sent?"*

And Mercy began to weep.—The thought that she has herself been called by the intervention of CHRISTIANA, makes this young beginner grieve over her relatives, who are still living in the midst of Destruction, no man caring for their souls. She is, however, comforted by the thought that this solicitude in their behalf may yet bring forth its fruits. Her tears and prayers and faithful efforts may yet be made the means of turning her friends and relatives to Christ.

The Slough of Despond.—This is represented as being in a worse condition than when CHRISTIAN overpassed it; and we know that it was then so deep and dangerous as to have well-nigh stayed his pilgrimage at the very threshold of the journey. This miry slough was continually undergoing repair, and yet was never thoroughly mended. To the ministry of the Word is entrusted the reparation of this deep place of conviction; and therefore much depends upon the materials used and the laborers employed. This is the place where conscience is troubled and the mind harassed with doubts and fears. It needs a sound ministry and true doctrine to conduct the soul across the deep morass, and also a thorough realization of the

---

*Romans 10:14–15—How then shall they call on him in whom they have not believed? and how shall they believe in him of whom they have not heard? and how shall they hear without a preacher? And how shall they preach, except they be sent? as it is written, How beautiful are the feet of them that preach the gospel of peace, and bring glad tidings of good things!

promises of God in Christ, which are supplied as "stepping-stones" across the slough. These promises CHRISTIAN had failed to seek for, and therefore found them not; but CHRISTIANA and her company fared better, for "they looked well to their steps," and so cleared the dangerous pass.

Dream out my dream by myself.—At this point the narrative assumes the style and manner of the former Allegory—the Dreamer directly dreaming the experiences of the Pilgrims. His informant now retires from the scene; the Dreamer's thoughts enlarge their scope, and already he sees the Pilgrim-company arrived at the Wicket-gate.

Christiana began to knock.—Still are the same conditions recorded on the Wicket-gate—"Knock, and it shall be opened unto you." And here occurs a test of faith, greater than was required of CHRISTIAN at this stage of his journey. Their knock at the Gate was answered, not by the immediate appearance of the porter, GOOD-WILL, but by the barking of a dog, to the great terror and discomfort of the timid Pilgrims. Here, again, is one of the wiles of the devil set forth for our admonition. He had sought to destroy CHRISTIAN by the dispatch of his fiery darts from the Castle; but GOOD-WILL did "pull him in." He now assails the feeble women and children with another kind of alarm, and again fails of his purpose, for the voice of GOOD-WILL doth effectually silence the dog, and bereave him of his power to hurt or harm the Pilgrims of the "narrow way."

But only CHRISTIANA and her children have entered; poor MERCY did still stand without. She had received the invitation of her companion, but she still needs the call of God. This is, again, one of the brilliant touches of the glowing pencil of the Dreamer. The poor, trembling suppliant, who still deems herself uncalled, unbidden, yet stands at the Gate, hoping for some kind message of mercy, some gracious token of acceptance; but this long, lingering delay doth sorely try and test her faith. CHRISTIANA, meanwhile, prays for her, in that power of intercessory prayer which God our Father vouchsafes to grant to the members of his great family. (James 5:16.)

Knocking at the gate herself.—Intercessory prayer is, no doubt, very helpful to the Christian; but we have not attained to the full power of prayer until we have taken that potent weapon into our own hands, and therewith knocked for ourselves at the door of grace. Thus it was with MERCY; weary of waiting, and anxious for admittance, she appeals, on her own account, by loud and repeated knocks, until the porter openeth to her also. And then—oh, what a sight! Behold a prostrate Pilgrim, the victim of her own doubts and fears, alarmed by her own loud call and claim upon the attention of the Master—fainting by the door of the Wicket-gate, which her own knock had opened! Oh, what strength is in the feeblest hand, what might in the weakest prayer, what life and future growth in the tiny seed of faith, though it be no greater than the grain of mustard seed! Surely, for some of the weak-hearted and feeble-minded of the flock is this delineation given. It is to such conscious weakness as this that Divine strength is vouchsafed. These fainting ones are revived and refreshed by the sweet-smelling myrrh and spices of the Spirit. "Thy comforts refresh my soul!"

Pardon by word and deed.—First, by the good promise of God, and then by the effectual work of Christ. We receive pardon, first by the assurance of the promise, and then by the sight of the Cross, and the spiritual view of the Crucified.

The dog.—The existence of danger so near to the Wicket-gate is a mystery to the mind of MERCY. The difficulty, however, is solved, when she is informed that the dog is Satan's property, kept there, close by the entrance-gate, to deter those that would go in thereat. And he would indeed deter them, but that a stronger than he delivers His servants from such fears and alarms of the pilgrimage.

The weather was comfortable.—This part of the road is pleasant; their lines have fallen unto them in a fair place. The relief is great, the promise of pardon is sure, and has already ensured to them the realization of the peace that pardon brings. They now sing the songs of their pilgrimage; and from this fair beginning they are enabled to anticipate what shall be the end of their journey.

Yet, not altogether without danger is this path of the Wicket-gate. The trees of the adjoining garden shot their branches over the wall of the narrow way, and presented their mellow and luscious fruits full in view of CHRISTIANA'S children. This was *their* temptation; and they plucked them, and did eat.

CHRISTIANA'S conscience is somewhat troubled by her children's conduct, and she reproves them, on the score that these fruits did not belong to them. Had the good woman known more, had she traced those fruits to the root that bore them, her voice had been lifted up more loud and more commanding, that her children should straightway forbear to eat. These fruits were *in* the narrow-way, but they formed no part of the King's possessions; the root of that tree grew in the garden of the Tempter, who threw these tempting baits over the very walls of salvation. These are the seductive pleasures and gaieties of life, those "youthful lusts" which war against the soul.

Two very ill-favored ones.—This danger tests the elder Pilgrims. Alone upon the highway, their virtue and innocence are assailed by those who would plunge them into sin and shame, and so recover them to the power of Satan. But virtue, though unprotected, is her own best protector. She first drops the veil of modesty over her face, and then resists with that native power that indignantly repulses the first approach of audacious violence, and continues to hold her own, while yet she cries aloud for help.

Their voice was heard.—Prayer calls to God for aid, and is always acceptable in his sight, whether it be the silent supplication, offered during the "still hour" of communion with his throne, or the sudden outcry of alarm, raised in the face of sudden danger. Never yet did an afflicted pilgrim cry unto the Lord, but some one of the army of relief has been dispatched to the scene of danger, to repulse the assailants and to deliver the suppliant. So was it now, in the present emergency.

This Reliever.—The conversation of this man discloses a hidden providence lurking beneath this danger. The women had forgotten their own weakness, and had omitted to ask for one stronger than they, to conduct them through the severe discipline of the Pilgrimage. The blessings and favors they had received at the Wicket-gate seem to have filled their firmament with sunshine; and so, they prepared not for the storms and tempests of the way. Accordingly, they must be practically taught how great danger they incurred by this neglect; and while they are yet near to the Gate, and within call of ready help, Providence permits this sudden peril to present itself; and, in the relief subsequently vouchsafed, reminds them of the oversight, and urges them instantly to repair the mistake.

It is in vain to excuse ourselves, as CHRISTIANA attempted to do, by saying that if it were necessary to have such help, God would have granted it. This is altogether to ignore the duty of prayer, and the responsibility that devolves upon us, of *asking* for such things as be needful. Surely, what is worth having, is worth asking for!

PART II.
CHAPTER III.

THE INTERPRETER'S HOUSE.

INTRODUCTION.—Once, again, we have arrived at the gate of the INTERPRETER'S House, and, under the guidance of the good INTERPRETER, we are about to be conducted through the "significant rooms" of this fair house, built for the refreshment and instruction of pilgrims. Those of our readers who expect to see such perfect pictures and lively representations as in the former visit, will, no doubt, be disappointed. The brilliant imaginings of the former description are not at all equaled by the subsequent delineation of this wondrous house. Bunyan seems to have poured forth his sublimest thoughts in his lucid pencilings of CHRISTIAN'S visit, and to have almost exhausted himself for any second attempt to create pictures and representations for the soul's instruction. The Dreamer seems, indeed, to be conscious of his failure to produce an effect as glowing and as grand as that of the former visit; for he introduces this apology, saying—"I choose to lead you into the room where such things are, because you are women, and they are easy for you."

Albeit the scenes of this second visit are not based on such grand conceptions, and lack that system and symmetry of arrangement which characterized the former view, we shall yet find scope ample enough for instruction in the things of God and of the soul. The service of Mammon described in the scene of the Muck-rake, and the power of energetic and trusting faith, indicated by the Spider, are both instructive scenes; the one representing the downward, and the other the upward, tendency of the soul, according as the heart is fixed on things above or on things beneath. The call and constant care of God are, after the fashion of one of Christ's own similitudes, beautifully set forth in the illustration of the Hen and her youthful brood. Here we also read other lucid representations—of patience under sufferings; the discharge of our rightful duty in our appointed place; the worthlessness of mere profession without fruits answerable thereto; and the inconsistency of carnal appetites with the fair-seeming externals of religion. These lively emblems are further strengthened and supported by the weighty aphorisms enunciated by the wisdom of the INTERPRETER, and are followed up by the experience of the Pilgrims, as related by them to the good man of the house, who sends them forth upon their way rejoicing, under the protection of the brave champion of the road, whose name is GREAT-HEART.

For the relief of Pilgrims.—To CHRISTIANA and her companions the INTERPRETER'S house was "a relief" in a double sense. (1) They had been alarmed and affrighted by the "ill-favored men" who had encountered them on the way; and now they enter this house of rest, for the purpose of peaceful retirement from the dangers of the outer road. (2) It was also for their relief, inasmuch as they there received those abiding helps, and gifts, and graces, and tokens of acceptance, which they so consistently retained even to their journey's end.

Christiana mentioned by name.—The tidings of this woman's conversion had been flashed on lightning wings all along the route of the pilgrimage, far in advance of her progress in the way, "There is joy in the presence of the angels of God over one sinner that repenteth."* They that turn to God are spoken of by angels, and rejoiced over too, as these heavenly messengers await the bidding of their Lord to go forth as ministering spirits, to minister to them that are the heirs of salvation (Hebrews 1:14). Her past unbelief is indeed well known, and how she sought to hinder CHRISTIAN in the way; but now these things shall be no more remembered against her; and rather is fulfilled in her the parable of the once disobedient son, who ignored his father's counsel, refused to obey his will, promised nothing but disobedience, and yet "afterwards repented and went," (Matthew 21:28–29).

His Significant Rooms.—These are the chambers of imagery, through which the INTERPRETER had conducted CHRISTIAN. And "significant" they are—of the ministry of the Word, of the power of indwelling sin, of the peace of Patience, and of the folly of blind Passion; significant, too, of the sustaining power of Divine grace, and the unction of the Spirit; significant of the good fight of faith; significant, also, of dark despair and of the scenes of final Judgment.

The muck-rake.—This is the first of the illustrations peculiar to CHRISTIANA'S visit. The crown celestial is proffered in exchange for

---

*Luke 15:10—Likewise, I say unto you, there is joy in the presence of the angels of God over one sinner that repenteth.

that implement of Mammon, that muck-rake of worldliness, and the offer is not only unheeded, but is not even recognized! Thus does the service of Mammon blind the eyes, and turn away the attention of the heart from the bright and glorious things of heaven. Ay, while we are, with an earthly mind, gathering the waifs, and strays, and worthless things that are borne on every breeze, all heaven is passing over us, and away from us, and beyond our reach, with its crowns and joys, and its eternal weight of glory.

The spider.—The meaning of this emblem does not at once occur to the minds of the Pilgrims; nor would it be likely to discover itself to our minds without the aid of interpretation. True faith is an active power. It climbs, notwithstanding the known infirmity of the flesh, and is not deterred, even by the felt venom of sin, from laying hold upon Christ, and seeking and finding an entrance into the very best room of his household.

The hen and chickens.—This is an emblem that has been honored by the Master's own selection, in his Divine instructions to his people (Matthew 23:37). The great point of the illustration here is in the allusion to the fourfold "call:"—(1) the "common call"—universal offer of the Gospel; (2) the "special call"—the moving influence of the Spirit; (3) the "brooding note"—the love and care of Jesus; and (4) the "outcry"—the alarm or admonition by which, in seasons of danger, we are recalled to the side of Jesus.

Let us see some more.—The Sheep led to the slaughter, and so patiently suffering its death, is an emblem of that patience under sufferings which it becomes all true children of God to exemplify, and of which Jesus was himself the great Exemplar.

The Garden of flowers is designed to teach us the importance of discharging well the duty of our station and calling; as members of one body, in which all the members have not, indeed, the same office, but each is honorable and honored in the fulfillment of his own vocation.

The Corn field, rendering back only straw and stubble as the fruit of the seed-time, represents the unfruitful recipient of God's grace and favor. What saith the Master?—"Cut it down; why cumbereth it the ground?"*

The Robin, with the spider in its mouth, is an emblem of the professor who makes a fair show of religion, and yet is dependent on his carnal appetites. This lovely-feathered bird, looking so innocent

---

*Luke 13:7—Then said he unto the dresser of his vineyard, Behold, these three years I come seeking fruit on this fig tree, and find none: cut it down; why cumbereth it the ground?

and fair, is yet degraded in its groveling tastes. It may soar aloft toward heaven, and sing its joyous song; but its food and nourishment are of the earth, earthy.

The Interpreter asked Christiana.—In the details of their experience, CHRISTIANA speaks with the boldness of a more advanced Pilgrim, while MERCY speaks with the becoming modesty of one who has but lately entered on the pilgrimage. She would be silent, if she could, until her experience is more enlarged. Not in visions and in dreams was she warned to flee from wrath; nor yet by the example of former Pilgrims, but by the invitation of CHRISTIANA, such as Moses gave to Hobab—"Come thou with us, and we will do thee good."*

The bath, etc.—The concluding events of this visit are full of deep spiritual significance, seeing that the opportunity is taken to invest CHRISTIANA and her company with those marks and credentials which CHRISTIAN had received at the subsequent stage of the journey—at the Cross and the Sepulcher. They are conducted to the bath, which Bunyan himself interprets, in a side-note, to mean, "the bath of sanctification." From thence they return washed and cleansed. They then receive the Seal of the Spirit; and, ere they leave the house, they are clothed upon with the Change of raiment—"fine linen, white and clean." Thus clad in the sanctifying righteousness of the Spirit, they are also "clothed with humility," each seeing the glory of the rest, and esteeming others better than themselves.

And now, as the last parting gift of the INTERPRETER, the Pilgrim band receive their convoy for the road, in the person of the indomitable GREAT-HEART, the future conductor of their pilgrimage, the hero of a hundred battles, the somewhat more than human GREAT-HEART—the boldest champion of the Second Part of the PILGRIM'S PROGRESS.

---

*Numbers 10:29—And Moses said unto Hobab, the son of Raguel the Midianite, Moses' father in law, We are journeying unto the place of which the LORD said, I will give it you: come thou with us, and we will do thee good: for the LORD hath spoken good concerning Israel.

PART II.
CHAPTER IV.

THE CROSS AND THE CONSEQUENCES.

INTRODUCTION.—All the Pilgrims of Sion must go by the way of the Cross. This is an indispensable stage of the journey. In the diverse operations of the Spirit, there may, however, be differences of administration even here; and these diversities receive an illustration in the experience of CHRISTIAN, and the after experience of CHRISTIANA, at this self-same stage. As a poor burdened sinner, still bowed beneath the weight of his sin, our former Pilgrim had advanced to this "ascending place," where stands the Cross of Jesus. At the sight—the spiritual perception of the Crucified One, his burden loosed from off his back, and fell into the open mouth of the Sepulcher. The Cross was to him "the place of deliverance;" conscience was there eased of its burden, and he received pardon and peace. But, in this second narrative, much of this deliverance had been already wrought during the preceding stages. More gradual was the process of pardon, until the Cross became the climax of that which had been begun at the Wicket-gate. From the mouth of GOODWILL (a Divine personage, as we have already observed) CHRISTIANA and her company received pardon by word, with the kiss of peace as the pledge and assurance of the promise. To this was, by-and-by, to be added a full view of the way in which this pardon was obtained, a distant prospect of which was showed them at the Wicket-gate. To the near view of that scene they have now arrived. They stand beside the Cross! This is to CHRISTIANA the full confirmation of her faith. CHRISTIAN had been so borne down, by his weight of guilt, and by his conviction of sin, that nothing but the view of the Cross and of the bleeding Lamb could suffice to loose those bonds, and set him free. And therefore Bunyan adds—"It was to give him a proof of the virtue of this, that he was suffered to carry his burden to the Cross." But in both experiences—of CHRISTIAN and CHRISTIANA, the CRUCIFIED ONE is honored and magnified, as the sinner's only hope; and both could alike say with Paul—"God forbid that I should glory, save in the Cross of our Lord Jesus Christ," Galatians 6:14.

And Great-heart before them.—The character of GREAT-HEART now begins to develop itself, in his double capacity as teacher and guide; for this brave man is mighty both in word and deed. There is something superhuman in the character of this great conductor of the pilgrimage. Mr. Scott's idea, that it means "the stated pastoral care of a vigilant minister," scarcely rises to the high dignity of this lion-hearted man. Nor can we agree with Macaulay in his charge of inconsistency against the Allegorist, in combining the teaching and militant office in this one personage.

In this double office of GREAT-HEART is certainly included more than can be found in any, even of the choicest and bravest human companions of the way. GREAT-HEART must rather mean a principle than a person—the Divine grace and boldness implanted in the heart, or kept so consciously near as to insure Divine protection and continual aid in all danger and necessities; that grace that makes the heart strong and lusty by feeding it with the daily bread of spiritual food. It is that Presence of Christ, so real and so near, that gives the Pilgrim conscious strength—such as Moses desired for his great enterprise, when he said, "If thy presence go not with me, carry us not up hence," Exodus 33:15.

Pardon by word and deed.—This is evidently a leading thought in the mind of Bunyan. He gives prominence to it at the Wicket-gate, and now more thoroughly unfolds its meaning at the Cross. Indeed, he labors to reveal its inner truth, and thereby to illustrate the mighty salvation obtained for us by Christ. We must, however, confess that this exposition of GREAT-HEART is not as lucid as most of the other doctrinal teachings of the Allegory; and we agree with Mr. Scott, when he says, "it is needlessly systematical and rather obscure." We might perhaps arrive at the same conclusion by stating the question thus—

Man once possessed an original righteousness, which consisted in his obedience to God. From this righteousness he fell by the sin of disobedience. A new covenant was straightway made with man, to this effect—if he can by obedience regain his former relationship to God, well; but if not, then, for the purpose of man's salvation the righteousness of another is offered, which is made available for man, and being perfect, is acceptable before God. To test man's power to regain his lost position by renewed obedience, a law was given, with legal righteousness attached to the perfect fulfillment of its conditions. Man has not kept this law; he has broken it, in thought, in word, and in deed. On the score, then, of man's own personal obedience, his salvation is utterly hopeless. Shall man die the death?

He need not; for now steps in the provision, in mercy made, of the righteousness of another—the righteousness of Christ. He is perfect God, and therefore righteous in all his ways, and holy in all his works. He is sinless man, and therefore righteous, needing no obedience to constitute his personal righteousness. But though he needed not such obedience, yet he *did* "learn obedience,"* and by his subjection to the law in all things, by his sinless submission to its demands, and by his sufferings as a substitute for man—he hath a righteousness which was not required or needed for himself, and which, as "the gift of righteousness," he hath now to bestow upon all those who will receive it by faith in his great sacrifice. This is the *deed*, by which pardon is attained—through the meritorious righteousness of Jesus, presented freely to us, by which we, who have no personal righteousness, are *accounted* righteous, through Christ's merits and for Christ's sake.

Simple, Sloth, and Presumption.—In the former pilgrimage we have read of these men—in their sin; we now read of them in their condemnation. Great sinners, who are zealous in their sin, and thus mislead those that would go right on their way, must be made examples of, that all men may see and take warning, that they follow not in their steps.

The Second Pilgrimage is conducted in the same way as was the former—exposed to, or exempt from, its difficulties and temptations, as God's good grace and mercy may appoint. Ofttimes the stumbling-block that has been in the path of one man has been removed ere the next pilgrim hies that way.

The hill Difficulty.—This hill is not a mere circumstance or incident, which may or may not occur upon the road, but is an essential part of the pilgrimage, and must be climbed, and thus overpassed. It is the next stage after the Cross, appointed as a test to those that have received pardon and peace, to see what they are able to bear and are ready to endure for Christ. It also is the stage before the communion of the Palace Beautiful, and is there placed, as an ordeal or sifting process, for trial and proof of faith; for only they who are prepared to combat with difficulties, and to overcome them, shall be accounted worthy of the more exalted privileges of the way.

But here is a drawback or disadvantage at the very base of the

---

*Hebrews 5:8—Though he were a Son, yet learned he obedience by the things which he suffered.

ascent: the spring of which CHRISTIAN drank, and by which he was refreshed, is now soiled and made muddy by the feet of some who are ill-disposed towards the Pilgrims of the Lord. This spring is the Word of God, in its refreshment of the soul. It was clear as crystal for the former Pilgrims, but not so now. Allusion is, no doubt, intended here to some degeneracy of spiritual life, and especially of spiritual teaching. This is the second allusion of the kind; a former instance being found at the Slough of Despond, which had been growing worse, owing to the indifferent materials used for mending it. It is supposed that during the interval between the writing of the two Parts of the PROGRESS, this declension had appeared in the ministers of the Word—their doctrine and teaching being not so pure as it had once been.

The advice here is goodly counsel—"Let it stand a while." Degenerate preaching of the Word is the admixture of error with truth, and as these elements cannot combine, they must be separated; and by-and-by the error will settle down by itself, and leave the waters pure. Then you may safely drink it, and be refreshed to meet the difficulties of the way.

The ascent, as its name implies, proved difficult. An interesting feature in the character of GREAT-HEART occurs here—his care of the little children. He is like the Good Shepherd that has love and tenderness enough to take the young lambs in his arms, and yet power and strength enough to slay the roaring lion that would devour the flock.

Within sight of the lions.—The experience of the path is unchanged, except in some few incidental circumstances. One of these incidents, that diversify the scene, is now before us. The pass of the lions seems even more dangerous now than it had been when CHRISTIAN passed that way. The lions are quite as wrathful; they are, moreover, backed by a Giant; the porter, WATCHFUL, is not in view; and the party consists of women and children. But, over against all these disadvantages, there is one countervailing advantage—they have brave GREAT-HEART with them; and this is everything.

This way had lain much unoccupied.—The political allusion here seems to be sufficiently apparent. The persecutions and disabilities of Bunyan's days had already deterred many from joining themselves in Christian fellowship, such as is indicated by the intercourse of the Palace Beautiful. The "lions" of persecution, backed by the "giant" hand of power, during that unhappy period, had desolated the highways of Christian communion, and driven back many from the companionships of the spiritual pilgrimage.

In the later days of Bunyan's life, the lions of persecution were "chained," that is, the persecuting laws were rendered inoperative; but the spirit of persecution (Giant GRIM) still remained, sufficient to deter the timid and faint-hearted ones from trying the pass. It needed but the vigorous effort of some GREAT-HEART of the period to clear the path for the liberty of after ages of the Church.

It is the King's highway.—GREAT-HEART lacks neither words nor deeds of greatness. He will enjoy for himself, and will have others to enjoy, the sweet communion of saints, and all other privileges of the people of God; and he enforces his demands because he is on the highway of the Lord his King. With a brave heart and a strong arm (now bearing only a spiritual interpretation) the journeying pilgrim of the road must be a hero in the strife, such as those great-hearted men of old, who stopped the mouths of lions, and laid grim giants prostrate on the battle-field.

PART II.
CHAPTER V.

THE PALACE BEAUTIFUL.

INTRODUCTION.—The sojourn in the Palace Beautiful, as described in the narrative of the former Pilgrimage, was characterized by all that was "lovely and of good report" in the provision and enjoyment of Christian privilege and opportunity. The second narrative well sustains the reputation of that fair house of godly communion and Christian fellowship. It is still, as before, a privilege so exalted as to be guarded by an ordeal of Difficulty in the entrance thereto, lest any unworthy pilgrims should cross that threshold of joy and peace. This chapter includes a lengthened review of Christian intercourse, sustained from day to day, to the comfort and edification of the Pilgrims. The nightfall, the weariness, and the danger, form a bold contrast to the home, the rest, and the safety here provided for the wayfaring company. Here God "giveth his beloved sleep," and dreams of heaven and blessedness play around them, while they repose in the peaceful chamber of their rest.

The scenes of this stage of the journey assume a more familiar character, and sometimes are so quaint as to be almost amusing. The catechizing of the children, and the ready answers of the boys; MERCY'S courtship with Mr. BRISK, and the sudden break off of the suitor's attentions; MATTHEW'S illness, its cause, and its cure by Mr. SKILL; the subsequent conversations; propounding of difficult questions; seeing of wondrous sights; and breathing of fervent farewells—all make up an interesting, entertaining, and instructive chapter of the Allegory of the Dreamer.

Dangerous traveling in the night.—Yes, even though GREAT-HEART is with them, as the brave conductor of the way. To the strongest and the best equipped there is no room for that bravado spirit that sees no danger and knows no peril. There are times when even GREAT-HEART is safer within the shrine of his great Master's house—seasons of darkness, the midnights that follow after our best and brightest days, during which we are reminded that we are not yet at home, but are still in the weary wilderness.

"I will return tonight."—Alas! evil tidings on the very threshold of enjoyment! GREAT-HEART is bidding them farewell! Having thus far conducted his company, he must now return to his Lord for fresh instruction and another mission. He has fulfilled the commission he had received at the INTERPRETER'S House—"Conduct them," said his Lord, "to the house called Beautiful." The Holy Spirit gives "grace by measure," and according to our asking. We must ask, and then we receive; we must ask for large things and for long-continued blessings, else we must not expect to receive largely. And herein was CHRISTIANA'S double mistake: in the first place, she had not asked at all; and in the next, she had not asked enough. Accordingly, at the outset she was granted no convoy for the road, and when she did receive the gift, it was but for a single stage—she had asked no more. Thus does God experimentally teach his children to feel their wants and to pray for needful supplies; and when they ask, he means that they should ask liberal things of him that giveth liberally, and upbraideth not.

What noise for gladness.—The greatness of their need is only equaled—perhaps surpassed, by the greatness of the welcome they receive. If men did but know the thousand welcomes that await them on the road to heaven, would they not gladly leave their sin, and follow Christ? All along the road are friendly greetings, Christian welcomes, and kindly gratulations. Thus the Pilgrims go on "from strength to strength," from stage to stage; and all along and everywhere they are entertained by the Lord of the Hill, who graciously provides helps, rests, and all other things that are necessary for the refreshment of the weary.

The great gladness expressed on this occasion was on account of the fact that, by the arrival of this company, the Christian family was completed. If there be joy in heaven over any one member that is brought to Jesus, there is greater joy when other members of the family follow, and yet greater gladness if the family circle is wholly given to Christ. Besides, the fair inhabitants of the palace had already taken an interest in CHRISTIAN personally, and had made special inquiries about his family. He had at that time no good report to give respecting them; but now his wife and children present themselves as candidates for the same communion of saints which CHRISTIAN had so largely enjoyed during his sojourn in this fair dwelling-place. This makes the damsels glad. All the graces of the Spirit are made stronger and more permanent, in proportion as they are enjoyed and cultivated in the genial atmosphere of the Christian home and family.

When they were at rest.—Upon their own petition they were permitted to choose the Chamber Peace, in which CHRISTIAN had slept during his visit to the palace. Bunyan has introduced a side-note here, which is suggestive of profitable thoughts. He writes—"Christ's bosom is for all pilgrims." Yes, the resting-place of the Christian is on Jesus' breast; that is, indeed, the Chamber of true Peace, where this soft pillow may be found on which to lay the aching head, and be at rest,—even upon our good Father's bosom.

Mercy, tell me thy dream.—MERCY dreams a dream, which contains, within a few sentences, the cross of many, and dissolves away into the glory of their crown. It was a dream well suited to the case of one like MERCY, who has been the only member of her family, as yet, to undertake the pilgrimage. Such lonely and solitary ones—witnesses for Christ in the midst of home discouragements—surely, they may take courage by the example of MERCY; her dream may be their reality. They are, perhaps, sore hindered in their way, laughed at, mocked, and ridiculed. This, no doubt, was MERCY'S case; this the cross she had to bear *at home*, else she had not dreamed this dream. But she sought Christian fellowship elsewhere, and found it in the company of her friend; and now enjoys a high festival of such holy gladness in the communion of the Palace. Here she seems to see the peculiar cross she has to bear, and how it changes into the crown of glory, as, in her dream, she is lifted to the throne of light; and she that finds no sympathy in her home on earth, now finds the sympathy of her home in heaven, and hears her heavenly Father's voice address her, saying—"Welcome, daughter!"

Stayed there about a month.—The communion of saints ought to be ofttimes enjoyed, or else, for a long time together. The heart has a natural tendency to decline from grace, and to decay in Christian strength. Christian intercourse is as the dew of heaven to the soul; it is as the fatness of the earth to the hidden root; it is as the supply of oil to the expiring lamp. Long continuance in these blessed opportunities is profitable to the soul's health and increase.

The catechizing.—This is designed not only to test the amount of the children's attainments in religious truth but also to test the faithfulness of CHRISTIANA, as a Christian mother, in the education of her children. Great responsibility devolves upon the mothers in our Israel, as to how they perform this great duty. Maternal influence is that which chiefly contributes to the formation of the habits of children; and, in a great measure, the spiritual education of the young belongs to a mothers care. In this case, CHRISTIANA had well discharged her responsibilities.

The *manner* of the catechizing is worthy of notice. PRUDENCE is the catechist. The questions proposed are adapted to the ages and capacities of the children. Beginning with the youngest child, and with the most elementary Christian truths, she advances to higher principles as she passes on to the elder boys. This is an important element in the art of catechizing. In examining as in teaching, the order must be—milk for babes, and strong meat for those of riper age and larger powers.

The *subject-matter* of the examination, also, demands attention. The questions are all on essential doctrines. The answers are prompt and ready, and pointed too, even to quaintness. The fundamental verities of the Christian faith are introduced even in the more elementary catechizing; and the youngest of the children is able to express himself on the subject of grace, and righteousness, and sanctification. Bunyan thus shows the importance of instructing even the youngest in the essentials of Christianity. He so sets forth the doctrine of the Trinity, and the offices of the Three Divine Persons respectively, as that even a little child should know them.

The progressive character of this catechizing conducts us from the simpler to the more abstruse subjects of Christian doctrine. For example: the youngest is examined in the plan of salvation, through the joint offices and individual work of the Trinity in Unity; the next in age is examined as to the nature of man and the philosophy of the scheme of redemption; the elder than he must tell somewhat respecting the world to come, and our relationship to its eternal destinies; while the eldest is catechized in the more abstract topics of religion—the nature of God, the character of the Bible, the limits of man's understanding, the necessity of Divine faith, concluding with a question and answer respecting the Resurrection of the dead.

PRUDENCE is pleased with the progress of the children, and commends them to the further care of their pious and devoted mother. They are to learn from the open book of Nature; but, above all, to receive their chiefest instruction from the unfolded book of God's Revelation to man.

Mr. Brisk.—This character introduces one of the amusing, but yet instructive, incidents of the narrative. This Second Allegory descends to the concerns of ordinary life, and, accordingly, includes a scene of courtship, in order to illustrate, in the person of Mr. BRISK, the choice of worldly wisdom, and, in the character of MERCY, how a Christian maiden determines to marry only "in the Lord." To young persons, this scene contains a pointed moral and a practical example worthy of being attended to.

Mr. BRISK is that character of young man, so often seen in society, that has discernment enough to know what constitutes a good housewife; and seeing in such an one as MERCY the combination of beauty, industry, and religion, determines to set his heart upon her, for the worldly gain that such connection seems to promise and insure. MERCY, perceiving these approaches, acts a wise part, by making inquiry respecting Mr. BRISK. The result is that she learns his character and aims. He thinks that this industry of MERCY is for the market of earthly gain; and when he is informed that, like Dorcas of old, this fair Christian maiden, having the root of faith, desires to be rich in good works and fruitful in godly labors, he has learned enough to prove that the spiritually-taught character of MERCY would but ill suffice to satisfy his greed of gain and worldly-wise policy. So he withdraws from the scene; and MERCY, by her consistent resolution, illustrates the counsel of the Word—"Be ye not unequally yoked together with unbelievers," 2 Corinthians 6:14.

Now Matthew fell sick.—Here, again, is a quaint scene, but true to the letter. It is also well told, and in full detail, after the fashion of the period. The moral is this—

MATTHEW was sin-sick: an internal disease had been engendered by some sin which he had committed, and by reason of which "the whole head was sick, the whole heart faint."

The cause of this sickness. Sin takes root in the heart and conscience, but does not always at the moment produce its evil results. Here, a season (how long, we know not, but an appreciable interval) had elapsed, so that at first it was hard to say what overt act or presumptuous deed had given cause to such disquietude. On inquiry, however, the bygone sin is brought to remembrance—the eating of the fruit of the trees that did overhang the way at the Wicket-gate. Sin is an evil seed, and, when planted, it springs up, sooner or later, prolific of its own bitter fruit.

The cure of the sickness. For the one cause of evil there is but the one remedy; and the cause being discovered by Mr. SKILL, he has but to apply this remedy. He first administers it in a weak and modified form, the allusion being to the remedy of the law, which was Christ in type and shadow, of use only to those who looked through the type to Christ, who was typified thereby. But the medicine of the law is weak; the strong and sufficient remedy must be found in Christ, revealed, manifested, and offered up for sin. Hence the potent cure prescribed is "the body and blood of Christ," spiritually received, as the balm for the sin-sick soul.

There is a graceful modesty in Bunyan's character displayed here. He records the prescription in Latin, after the fashion of physicians; but, being himself illiterate in this world's learning, he apologizes for the use of these Latin words, observing in a side-note: "The Latin I borrow"—an incident illustrating the genuine spirit of the man.

There is much spiritual significance in the sequel—the manner of taking this spiritual prescription, the mingling of the medicine in the "tears of repentance," the loathsomeness of the remedy to MATTHEW'S carnal taste, the urgent necessity of the case, the authoritative tone of the physician, the touch of nature in the scene when CHRISTIANA tastes the supposed nauseous thing, and pronounces it to be "sweeter than honey"—all this contains deep meaning, suggestive of most profitable reflections to thoughtful minds.

Then Matthew asked her.—PRUDENCE, who had been the examiner, is now appealed to as a teacher. Significant questions elicit equally significant answers:—

(1) CHRISTIANA'S own motto is brought to mind here—"The bitter must come before the sweet, and that also will make the sweet the sweeter." The discipline of the Word of God is against the grain of the carnal heart, but is good for the soul's health and wellbeing.

(2) The natural heart is filled with all manner of spiritual uncleanness. The Word of God is the medicine of the soul, rendering the corrupt heart pure and holy, meet dwelling-place of a righteous God.

(3) The sun is the source of light; its rays are diffused over all the globe, descending in a flood of glory. Such is the fullness of God's gift of light to the world. But earthly fire rises, as though it would return to its birth-place. Hence the ascending fire of the altar and the smoke of the incense coiling upward to the skies, are used in Scripture as the emblems of prayer and thanksgiving, Psalm 141:2. But how faint are the fires of our sacrifices, and how few our pillars of incense, in comparison with the full and omnipresent sun-light of heaven!

(4) The fullness of the ocean flood is derived from the rains of heaven; and in the mists and evaporations the waters of the earth do but render back a portion of the gift they have received—the springs, and rivers, and rich harvests, and other gifts, being the blessings that they leave behind.

(5) The rainbow is caused by the conjunction of sunshine and rain. It is the emblem of hope—nature's sunshine amid nature's tears. Without the cloud it could not be seen, and without the sun it could not appear.

(6) The waters of the great deep are filtered for our use through the earth, and are thus adapted for the use of man. So is the glory of Jehovah revealed to us through the earthly body of Jesus, and through his human sorrows and sufferings we receive "the grace of God, which bringeth salvation,"

(7) Not only are the low-lying valleys watered with refreshing streams, but also high upon the hills do springs of waters break forth. God visits all sorts and conditions of life with the joys of his salvation. There are lofty mountains that send down their streamlets to the valleys; and so are there great, and rich, and mighty men, who use their Christian influence aright, in serving their generation and doing good to their fellow-men.

(8) The wick of a candle is to consolidate the light and to prevent its burning out too suddenly or too soon. The candle thus burns regularly and on system, and gives light to the end of its course. True religion must not be a mere flash of momentary impulse, but a steady-burning and shining light in the soul.

(9) And as the candle burns, it needs to be fed and nourished. The material that surrounds it is its food; and as it gives light on system, so on system it receives its food.

(10) There are in nature many illustrations of the Divine mystery of godliness: the faint echoes of creation responding to the voice that called it into being, evidences that before the foundation of the world, the scheme of redemption, by the shedding of the blood of Christ, had been fore-ordained and appointed.

(11) So also are these natural emblems of Divine lessons. The cock-crowing, for instance, serves to remind us of many profitable reflections, associated with the examples of those that have gone before, as well as with the duties that now devolve upon ourselves.

Now their month was out.—Thus did the Pilgrims spend the period of their sojourn; and now it was time to arise and go forward, and once more to face the dangers of the way. In the anticipation of their need, they are reminded of the departure of GREAT-HEART, and that he may be fetched back again only for the asking. Accordingly, they forward a petition to the INTERPRETER that he would renew his grant of GREAT-HEART, still to be the conductor of the pilgrimage, even to the end; and their prayer is granted.

PART II.
CHAPTER VI.

THE VALLEY OF HUMILIATION.

INTRODUCTION.—This chapter includes, as though in one day's march, several consecutive stages of the former Pilgrimage. The company now proceed downwards to the continuously descending valleys—first to the Valley of Humility, thence to the Valley of Humiliation, thence deeper down to the Valley of the Shadow of Death. They thus walk the selfsame ground that CHRISTIAN had trod before them, and are enabled to recognize on the way some few memorials of his struggles and his victories. But how altered are these stages of the journey! Where CHRISTIAN had walked in the way of hard experience, these Pilgrims reap the benefit of his example—avoiding the slips and snares that he experienced, and walking in safer places under the guidance of their brave conductor. Under these favorable circumstances, the whole character of the valley is rendered, not only easy to pass through, but even desirable to dwell in. It is the abode of peace and plenty and loveliness. Lilies grow upon its surface, and sheep are browsing on its grassy mead. Here the shepherd-boy sings his pastorals; and all its pilgrims are "clothed with humility." In such a place as this, no doubt, they would build to themselves habitations, and dwell therein. But this cannot be; they must pass through it, and out of it—into a lower valley still.

The Valley of the Shadow of Death now opens to their view, and GREAT-HEART leads the way. This valley is still filled with horrors; but it is less perilous to our present Pilgrims, because it is day, and the sun shines upon their path, and their dauntless guide is with them. Still, darkness suddenly descends, and intercepts their progress; and, like CHRISTIAN, they are made to feel the necessity and power of prayer; for, on the descent of darkness, they pray for light, and, lo, the blessed light of heaven doth again encompass them.

The Valley of Humiliation.—Once more we are introduced to the *dangerous* descent of the *difficult* hill. Difficulties and dangers, however, are greatly mitigated in the case of CHRISTIANA and her companions. Even here, though the descent was steep and slippery (as it always is), this company of Pilgrims, with care and caution, got down safely.

It is important to observe the position in which the Lord of the hill has thus caused to be built this fair house of his—the Palace Beautiful, the abode of Christian communion and fellowship. At one side there is difficulty, in climbing to its elevation; this is so designed as to render Pilgrims conscious of their urgent need. At the other side, there is danger, in descending from its sublime enjoyments; this is also designed for a purpose—to suggest the need of caution, and to furnish scope and opportunity for putting forth and using the supplies of spiritual strength that have been received. This is illustrated in the narrative of both Pilgrimages—though differently in each.

Intimation of the reason.—The manner of accomplishing this descent is the measure of the danger of the valley itself. CHRISTIAN had many slips by the way; and hence the hard experience he met with in his fight with APOLLYON. He that walks not steadfastly, after enjoying the great privilege of Christian fellowship, may well expect to meet with some sharp brunt that will teach him to walk more circumspectly, and more dearly prize the strength he has received.

The best and most fruitful ground.—It is plain it is something within ourselves, and not in the nature of the valley itself, that doth cause us to meet with hardships in the vale. It is a prolific ground, producing fruits and flowers in rich and rare abundance—meet emblem of the spirit of humility, that spiritual soil that is most productive of Christian virtues and heavenly graces. We are spiritually nearer to God, and more like to Christ, while dwelling in the low-lying valley of humility, or even in the still lower valley of humiliation, than when perched upon the mountain-top of human pride. The mountain-summit may be covered with the chill and icy barrenness of the everlasting snows, while in the well-watered valleys beneath are the abounding fruits, and sweet-scented flowers, and waving corn-fields of a garden which the Lord hath blessed.

The shepherd-boy's song.—This is one of the purest gems of the Allegory—the scene of the shepherd-boy, singing his pastoral song of humility, while he feeds his father's sheep. The peace and quietude of the valley, the joy and gladness of the spirit of the swain, the beauty and pathos of the song he sings, and, above all, the contrast with the experience of CHRISTIAN in this same valley—all tend to enhance the sublimity of the occasion, and to point out how happy, thrice happy, are those humble-minded and lowly Pilgrims whose hearts are in accord with the spirit of the place. Oh, for more of the spirit of humility! for more of that mind that was in Christ Jesus! for in this valley was the chosen resort of the Savior. Yes, in the lowly peace, and shade, and quietude of this deep vale, did the Son of the Highest dwell for a space; and he who would be as Christ was, will also seek his habitation there. So near is the footstool of humility to the throne of glory!

Forgetful Green.—The cause of CHRISTIAN'S hard experience in this valley receives here additional illustration. Besides his "slips" in the descent of the hill, there was yet another cause of offence—his departure from the right way, by which he wandered into the place of Forgetfulness. The dispensation of Providence to the Pilgrim had been a dispensation of favor and goodness. The Author of these blessings was ever to be remembered, never to be forgotten; more particularly after the large and liberal favors bestowed upon him in the communion of the Palace. Yet it would appear that this was a moment of forgetfulness, a season of oblivion of God's goodness, while CHRISTIAN traversed the valley, and that therefore he met with that fierce encounter and that long-continued conflict, so that he might again be taught to know and recognize the hand that hitherto had been over him for good, guiding and guarding him in his Pilgrimage.

This is the place.—The realization of previous downfalls and reverses may be as admonitory to the Pilgrims as the review of successes would be encouraging. Memorials of the conflict remain long after the battle has concluded, long after the champions have ceased to fight. God, in his providence, permits the marks and tokens of the fray to abide, as an evidence of the intensity of the strife, and a proof of the greatness of the victory. Veteran heroes generally show their scars and wounds, as tokens of many a hard-fought battle, and of many a campaign through which they have passed. This battle-field was, indeed, a part of the valley into which CHRISTIAN ought not to have ventured; but from the moment he was recalled to the remembrance of his God and Father, all his wounds were proofs of the genuineness of his fidelity and of the power of his faith—evidences that he would not be brought into bondage of the Destroyer.

The Shadow of Death.—"This doleful place," though not utterly dark, was yet dismal enough to our Pilgrim-company. The intense horror of the place was much moderated on this occasion; for GREAT-HEART was with the Pilgrims. Dangers arise; fiends appear; groans are heard; earthquakes rumble beneath their feet; and serpents and scorpions, with a hissing sound, alarm them. Thus do spiritual misgivings crowd upon the soul, and at times startle the spirit of true Pilgrims. Convictions, doubtings, fears, lay siege round about the spiritual man, and, more or less, disturb his peace, weaken his faith, and darken the prospect of his hope. Even with the company of GREAT-HEART, these troubles came upon these Pilgrims; but when they kept close to his protecting hand, and set his great strength in advance, the danger vanished.

Great-heart went behind.—Here is the protecting providence of Divine favor once more screening the Pilgrims from assault. At one time it goes before them, at another time it follows them—always standing between the Pilgrims and the harm that is designed against them. Like the pillar of cloud in the wilderness—it acts both as a protection and a guide.

A great mist and a darkness.—Dangers thicken now around the feet of the Pilgrims. Some dark moment of spiritual fear is indicated here, the darkness increasing the effect of their other sorrows. Even GREAT-HEART seems as though he were brought to a stand-still at this dark spot; and, having large experience of the way, he suggests the use of that potent weapon by which CHRISTIAN had been delivered in his deepest and darkest extremity—the weapon of All-prayer. "So they cried and prayed." God will not conduct them out of that dark place without being inquired of concerning these things.

Their need is felt; their prayer is offered; the prayer is heard; yea, it is answered—"and God sent light and deliverance!"

Maul, a giant.—The former narrative places the cave of Giants POPE and PAGAN at the end of this valley. In this Allegory another giant is represented as issuing forth from this same cave. The name of this giant is MAUL. This new enemy is supposed to mean some vigorous State persecution, which, in persecuting policy and power, may be said to have taken the place of the former giants of the place. Bunyan's own day, alas! experienced the hand of power and the "club" of persecution: and it needed such a one as GREAT-HEART to breast the impetuous waves and stay the tide of wrath. And, in God's mercy, those days were shortened. And while great-hearted men stood forth as the defenders of the weak, and engaged in mortal combat against the persecuting statutes of the period, the weaker ones stood by, as CHRISTIANA and her children did, and watched the issue of the fight; until, by-and-by, the faith and steadfastness of a noble few opened the gates of liberty to all; and, thank God, those gates of freedom have never since been utterly closed, at least in these lands.

PART II.
CHAPTER VII.

MR. HONEST AND MR. FEARING.

INTRODUCTION.—Mr. HONEST and Mr. FEARING are two characters magnificently drawn by the skill of the Dreamer, who has thereby set before his readers two very sublime descriptions of men of God—characters, however, which are essentially unlike, except in just one point of similitude—that they were both Pilgrims, with their faces Sionward.

In Mr. HONEST we have obtained a new companion, whose intercourse will greatly enliven the story. He is a hero, possessed of a true heroic spirit; he is a fatherly man, possessed of a paternal spirit, quaint and playful in his style and manner, and one who is welcomed by the Pilgrims, young and old, as a real acquisition to their little company. He is well acquainted with the road, has met with many pilgrims, and has large experience of the way. He continues with the Pilgrim-band to the end of the journey, and performs some brave exploits in the course of the pilgrimage.

The description of the character of Mr. FEARING is one of the most complete successes of the Dreamer's inimitable genius. He was not a hero, but he was not a coward; he had the fear of God before his eyes, but of his fellow-man he had no fear. Here is the blending of true humility and humbleness of soul with earnest zeal for God's glory. Mr. FEARING was a timid, fearful, half-desponding man, retiring and unobtrusive in his ways; always ready to believe with trembling, but never once guilty of presumption; a sensitive soul, shrinking at the merest touch, from the tenderness of his conscience.

They went to the ascent.—The same standpoint from whence CHRISTIAN had espied FAITHFUL in the distance, now serves as a place of rest, and for purpose of refreshment, after the hard encounter of GREAT-HEART with Giant GRIM, and the painful anxiety of the Pilgrims as to the issue of the conflict. At this point, too, where CHRISTIAN had sought for fellowship and communion, our present Pilgrims enjoy this privilege; he was but one, and they are many.

So, they take occasion to talk of the late mercy and deliverance vouchsafed to them, and are thankful.

An old Pilgrim, fast asleep.—This is old Mr. HONEST, who is now, for the first time, introduced to our notice. Whether this was a time and place allowed for sleep, we cannot well decide. He certainly awaked with a shock of fear, as though from a forbidden or unlawful slumber; and yet his conscience does not seem to have been at all uneasy, for he begins to testify wherein is his confidence, and what would be his conscious strength in case of any assault by the bandits of the way.

What would you have done?—Mr. HONEST is a brave old Pilgrim. His bold speech, in answer to GREAT-HEART'S question, at once shows what style of man he is, and seems rather to amuse the great warrior-guide. They are two like-minded men: very brave, very trustful, and therefore very joyous.

My name I cannot.—This good man is not presumptuous or proud. His spirit of humility is apparent from the first. He deems his name to be too good for him, and better than his nature; and lest he should seem to make undue pretensions by parading his name, he chooses rather to tell his origin, which is not so fair or flattering. We are thus informed that he is not one of the wise, mighty, noble, or learned, but that he is (as others may be) "honest" for all that. He does not forget the rock from which he was hewn, nor the hole of the pit from whence he was digged. Out of the same region as Destruction, and from no very promising pedigree, has he proceeded. He feels, however, the great spiritual change that has been wrought in his soul; and when GREAT-HEART tells him he knows it all, Old HONEST "blushes to find it fame."

Your name is Old Honesty.—And when GREAT-HEART does name his name, it is somewhat higher and more honorable than even that by which he calls himself. "Not Honesty in the abstract," says the good old man, showing that he has learned some of the science of Christian philosophy since he left the town of "Stupidity." And he is right. Honesty in the abstract would mean the possession of that virtue in perfection and in all its power; but "Honest" means that he is aiming to attain that goodly characteristic.

And this man's change was indeed a great one: from a state worse than that of Destruction itself, farther removed from the Sun of Righteousness, and yet (oh, great miracle of grace!) the light-bearing, life-giving rays of the Light of the world penetrated even to that cold, dark, senseless place, and warmed the heart of this man into love to God in Christ.

One Mr. Fearing.—We do well to give heed to the description of this man's spiritual character. It illustrates another phase of spiritual life. He was known to Mr. HONEST, but much better known to GREAT-HEART, who had been the convoy of his pilgrimage, as he now is of CHRISTIANA'S company. From GREAT-HEART'S description of this worthy Pilgrim, we are enabled to obtain a very picture of the man and of his spiritual state; and the whole scene forms a study in itself for the Christian man—a combination of natural weakness and of spiritual strength; of constitutional depression, and yet of holy determination that, come what may, he would still hold on to his pilgrimage. We will follow GREAT-HEART'S review of this man's strangely chequered career in its successive stages—

At the Slough of Despond: Here he would be peculiarly liable to suffer loss, his own nature being in such near conformity to the spirit of this miry place. Even a straw would suffice to stumble him; and where a more sanguine spirit would see a possibility of escape, he could see none. His soul refused to be comforted. Despond was not merely a stage of his pilgrimage, but the very type of the man himself.

At the Wicket-gate: The entrance-gate of the Narrow-way is a place of promise and command—"Knock, and it shall be opened unto you." Yet, here he hesitated to obey the command, and therefore so long postponed the enjoyment of the promise. Such a one, in the depression of his heart, has no boldness; he fears to knock, or to arouse the Master; and when at last he does knock, it is with so feeble a hand as scarcely to be heard. Yet the ear of the porter at the gate is quick to catch the faintest sound of the inquiring sinner; and to these trembling ones he speaks words of peace, and presents an open door of pardon and acceptance.

At the Interpreter's house: To this house of call he had an invitation and a note of introduction, and yet he feared to enter or to ask the favors he required. Here the INTERPRETER (the Holy Spirit) "helpeth his infirmities," and pours out the abundance of his love towards him; and, because the man is lowly and abased, the Spirit welcomes him the more, pours consolation into his bosom, reassures his doubting heart, and also provides GREAT-HEART as his conductor.

At the Cross: His fearful spirit was refreshed as he lingered beside the Cross and the Sepulcher. Kindred sympathies were awakened in his breast as he contemplated that scene of the Savior's sufferings. The great love of Jesus, the cross and passion, the blood of Christ, the agony and the death of the great Sacrifice—these topics revive and refresh his spirit; for this good man did love the Savior with devoted love, though with a weak power of faith.

At the hill Difficulty: Here he felt no such drawbacks as other Pilgrims had encountered. His fears were not earthly fears, but spiritual; not about his body, but about his soul. Therefore the "lions" of persecution alarmed him not. His fear was for the safety of the jewel, not of the setting; for the pearl of great price, not of the earthen casket that contained it.

At the house Beautiful: His constitutional diffidence still haunts him, and restrains him from the free interchange of Christian communion. He fears to make an open profession of religion, or to raise expectations as to his own spiritual state; and yet he longs to hear the conversation of those that fear his much-loved Savior. He therefore, rather by stealth than openly, listens to the sweet communion of the palace, and is comforted.

In the Valley of Humiliation: This would seem to be his native air and the abode of his choice; and, accordingly, here he was perfectly at home and at ease. He loved the deepness of this low-lying vale, its quietude and its peace. Here he could indulge the spirit of lowliness, and rejoice to say, as the Psalmist said—"My soul is even as a weaned child," Psalm 131:2.

In the Valley of the Shadow of Death: This would be the crisis of the fears of such a fearful and faint-hearted man. Here are spiritual dangers—those that most of all were the terror of his soul. Yet see the goodness of the Lord in measuring out the proportion of discipline to his sensitive and fearful children! The Valley was still and quiet—no dread visions of darkness and of the deep; no strong assaults of the Evil One. Demons and devils were restrained in their dens that day, till Mr. FEARING had overpassed the valley. Oh ye feeble-minded men! be strong, be comforted! God hath not forgotten you; he will be better to you than all your fears.

In Vanity Fair: Here, again, his fears are proved not to have been carnal fears—of man or of earthly things. In Vanity Fair, and in his intercourse with its vain inhabitants, he was bold as a lion, reproving and rebuking the men of the fair and their vain and profitless vanities. He had not the fear of man before his eyes, but ever lived as in the sight of God, his conscience ever tender, his heart ever fearful, lest he should in anywise offend, and so lose his acceptance at the last.

At the fords of the River: His fears were at all times great; but the provisions of God's grace were in proportion large. Once more, the way is made easy before him, and, in the passage of the River of Death, God's good mercy is upon him. Instead of depths to pass through, he has shallows to wade in; instead of troubles answerable to his fears, he is assured that all is well at last; and thus, without a pang, and in fuller assurance than he had ever felt before, he passed the fords of the river almost dry-shod, and entered into joy, and peace, and rest.

This is, indeed, a marvelous picture of a true Pilgrim—with love so warm, to have fears so great; so loving and so humble, and yet so doubtful and desponding! His lack of confidence in himself prevented his full enjoyment of Christian privilege. He looked, perhaps, too much to his own unworthiness, and too little to the worthiness of Christ. His sadness chequered his sunshine; his tears obscured his clearer vision; the clouds hung too low upon the mountains of his joy. Ere he had realized his hope and confidence, a shadow would intervene and rob him of his peace—

> "And in that shadow I have passed along,
> Feeling myself grow weak as it grew strong,
> Walking in doubt, and searching for the way,
> And often at a stand—as now, today."

Yet, notwithstanding, his faith in Christ was true. Like the needle that ever points, yet always tremblingly, to the pole, so did this poor man, with fear and trembling, ever tend and always look to Jesus his Savior.

The imperfection of Mr. Fearing.—Diverse are the characteristics of pilgrims; some sorrowful, some rejoicing; some desponding, others glad of heart. It may be that Wisdom is justified of all these her children; but it would not be to the profit of the Church if all men were like this Mr. FEARING. If it were so, there would be no Christian joy, or hope, or happiness; and the children of the King would go mourning all their days, shrinking from both privilege and duty, as though they were but half-trustful of Divine providence and grace.

Mr. Self-will.—As a contrast to the humble spirit of Mr. FEARING, the presumption of Mr. SELF-WILL is now set forth. This was a self-righteous man, who sought to balance his virtues against his vices, to be a servant to sin and righteousness at the same time, and to build his house partly on the rock and partly on the sand. He quotes other men's sins as the warrant of his own offences; and where others have been overtaken in a fault, he cultivates their sin into a system, and deliberately walks in the way of transgression. Surely, the conscience of this self-willed professor must be seared, and insensible to the hardest contact. No man's sins can by any means be allowed to give sanction to sin, or be used as a justification of wrong-doing by others.

Time enough to repent.—Procrastination is said to be "the thief of time," and so, in a spiritual sense, it may be said to be "the thief of souls." If we are to be "rooted and grounded" in love, ere we are fit for heaven, we do well to plant the seed early, and allow time for the growth of both root and branches. Suffice it to say, there is no time to lose, no time to trifle with. If eternity is the unending period of bliss, surely this brief span of time cannot be too long for all the work we have to do, for all the talents we have to use, for the attainment of the heavenly character, and for that growth in grace, and conformity to the image of Christ, without which no man shall see the Lord.

PART II.
CHAPTER VIII.

THE GUESTS OF GAIUS.

"How quickly strife and envy end,
   How soon all idle griefs depart,
When friend takes counsel thus with friend,
   When soul meets soul, and heart meets heart.

"We have so many things to say,
   So many failings to confess,
Time flies, alas! so soon away,
   We cannot half we would express."

INTRODUCTION.—CHRISTIAN companionships constitute breaks in the pilgrimage and intervals of rest to the Pilgrims. These occasions are not all of like spiritual importance. We have already seen how the Palace Beautiful was opened to the Pilgrim-band. Here the gifts and graces of the Spirit were personified and represented; but now a more familiar scene opens to our view: the entertainment of the company by a brother Christian, who is supposed to receive all true Pilgrims, and to refresh them for their onward progress—indicating the ordinary intercourse of fellow-pilgrims one with another. Accordingly, our author here forsakes his usual allegorical style of nomenclature, and, from a Scriptural allusion, derives the appellation of the man who entertains the Pilgrims, calling him by the name of GAIUS—a name appropriately bestowed, in allusion to the Apostle's message—"Gaius mine host, and of the whole Church, saluteth you," Romans 16:23.

Here, again, the little group enlarges, by the addition to their number of MR. FEEBLEMIND and MR. READY-TO-HALT; and these twain Pilgrims, like MR. HONEST, continue with the company to the end of the journey. The introduction of MR. FEEBLE-MIND to the group furnishes an illustration of the importance of joining, hand-in-hand, in faithful effort to rescue men of failing strength (as they may be rescued) out of the hands of the Destroyer.

Wished for an inn.—There is an evident difference indicated here between the provision of special means of grace and the more ordinary occasions of Christian instruction and fellowship. The former has been already set forth in the representation of the Palace Beautiful; and now one of the stated and appointed opportunities of the communion of saints is more particularly alluded to, where we meet, not so directly with the graces of the Spirit in themselves, as with our fellow-Christians, who exemplify those graces in their own experience. This is one of the constituted rights and privileges of the Christian man during the course of his pilgrimage—to give and to receive the blessings of brotherly or ministerial intercourse and fellowship.

They went in, not knocking.—A sense of freedom and a consciousness of right seem to be associated with this introduction of the Pilgrims to the House of GAIUS—a house which (it is to be observed) is represented as an "inn," not as a private residence; a place into which they could enter by right, and not by special favor only, and for pay or reward, as will appear at the close of the visit. The only qualification needed for admission is that they be "true Pilgrims." It is possible the double meaning is a correct one—a Christian household, at times enlarged into a congregation, by the admission of those who are true and sincere followers of the same Savior. Such households were familiar to Christians in Bunyan's day, as they certainly were also in the apostolic age, when "the Church in thy house" was included in the apostolic salutations (See Romans 16:5; 1 Corinthians 16:19; Philemon 2). In the one aspect, admission to the house would be a matter of personal favor, and, in the other, a matter of Christian duty. Both phases are here combined; for we cannot afford to lose either on the one hand the idea of this good man's hospitality, or, on the other, the freedom and right of entrance assumed by the Pilgrim-party.

And, consistently with this idea, we find in the person of GAIUS both a minister and a friend. He instructs them; he feeds them, after a spiritual sort—with food suited to the age and experience of each. He feeds the younger children with "milk," the elders with "butter and honey." He gives them the "apples" of the Lord's love, and then, "nuts," the more hidden and difficult doctrines of the faith, that must be broken up in order to find the kernel. All this is emblematic teaching. GAIUS also interests himself, as minister and friend, in family arrangements, by his counsel and advice. And again, more after the duty of a congregation than of an individual household, the Pilgrims go forth to destroy the Giant SLAY-GOOD; and thereby their little group enlarges in number, and is made to include the weak as well as the strong, so that they that are strong may, by Christian communion and sympathy, "bear the infirmities of the weak."

The readiness of GAIUS to supply the (spiritual) wants of this company is worthy of observation. Without notice of any sort, even without knocking at the door, the Pilgrims had presented themselves for food and refreshment; and, lo! it is ready. How important is this mark of true ministerial worth—this readiness to speak a word in season to them that are weary, and out of the overflow of the heart's abundance to bring forth things new and old, sufficient for the wants of those that need!

On the behalf of women.—Christianity has ennobled and exalted woman. Heathendom has degraded her; and even Judaism restricted her rights. Wherever the effects of the Fall are unrepaired and unrestored, woman still feels the full share of her own condemnation for the fatal part she played in the dread tragedy of Eden. But if woman was "the first in the transgression," she was also made the vehicle of the fulfillment of the promise of the coming Savior, who was to be "the seed of the woman." And, accordingly, ever since the Second Adam, "born of a woman," restored that which our first mother forfeited, the original dignity and glory of woman has been rendered back again; and throughout all Christendom, and during all the ages of the Christian faith, woman has had honor laid upon her, after the example of the holy women who adorned the doctrine of Christ their Savior, and thereby helped to establish woman's claim to that reverence, honor, love, and admiration, which they universally receive in all Christian lands.

Yes, the women that followed Christ have imparted a grace and a glory to the Gospel narrative which had been utterly wanting were men the only actors in the scenes of the Savior's life and ministry. How they wept their tears of penitence, and washed his feet in the lowliness of their humility, and wiped them with the flowing tresses of their hair! How diligently Martha served him; how earnestly Mary heard him; how devotedly the Magdalene loved him! When strong men who had strength to fight, forsook him and fled, the weak women of Galilee, with nothing but their heart-love to sustain them, followed the Master through all, even to the last. They saw him die; they followed him to his burial; they prepared sweet spices to embalm the body of their Lord; and they that lingered the longest to see the dark sunset upon Calvary, were the first privileged to see the glorious sun-rise of the Easter morning; for it was to the several groups of women, who were early at the sepulcher, that Jesus did first manifest himself after his Resurrection.

So supper came up.—The thoughts and reflections of the company are suggested by the circumstances of the occasion. The preparation for the feast is not the festival. The cloth, and the trenchers, and the trappings are not the *food* that satisfies the hungry soul. There may be the fire and the wood; but, "where is the lamb?"—that is the question, which only our "Jehovah-Jireh" can sufficiently answer! Amid all our preparations and preliminaries, let us not forget that Jesus is "the bread of heaven," and from his Spirit alone can proceed "the water of life" to the strengthening and refreshing of our souls. And, after we have been fed, as pilgrims, with heavenly food, we shall enjoy a richer banquet and a nobler feast, when, our pilgrimage ended and our journey done, we shall eat of the corn of the better country, and of the milk and honey of the Promised Land, and sit down with Abraham, Isaac, and Jacob, in our Father's kingdom.

Mr. Honest began to nod.—The weak and feeble members of the flock seem to be allowed the rest and refreshment of sleep during the period of Christian intercourse; but they are under protection and in a safe place while they sleep. The strong men, however, are not permitted this indulgence; and, therefore, when MR. HONEST shows signs of drowsiness, he is kept awake by the conversation of GAIUS. It is here, as it was with CHRISTIAN and HOPEFUL on the Enchanted Ground—if they would keep themselves awake, it must be by the same "saints' fellowship," and communing on the things of God. Accordingly, GAIUS continues the conversation.

A story worth the hearing.—This is a parable, with a moral attached. The trial of our faith depends very much upon the circumstances of our lot; and the faith that is most approved before God is that which resists the carnal nature, and fights the good fight, and overcomes at the last. True faith is that vital influence that conquers living temptations, not dead ones; subduing the legion of warring desires, and destroying the living seeds of sin in the heart.

If we can do any good.—Here is the family-circle, enlarged to a congregation of believers, addressing itself to useful labor in its own locality—going forth in the strength of its faith to see if it can do any good. Christian congregations must not monopolize the blessings of the Gospel, but spread them abroad to others. Like stars, we are not only to receive light, but also to reflect light. Sometimes opportunities are put in our way for doing good, and sometimes for preventing evil. In one place an "open and effectual door" may be set before us; and in another, some giant impediment—some modern SLAY-GOOD, may have to be removed ere the Gospel-words' work can enter. There is ample scope and work enough for all.

There are some who say that by the "giants" of the PILGRIM'S PROGRESS, Bunyan always means to indicate the persecuting power of the period in which his lot was cast. This may be so; but it does not exclude other interpretations. For example: this fierce Giant, though slain by GREAT-HEART, lives still in his posterity. Many a SLAY-GOOD still holds in bondage many a FEEBLE-MIND, furnishing fields of labor to those that would go forth to seek for work in the great Master's cause. No expedition of this kind, if undertaken and carried out in the proper spirit, can be without some good results; some feeble-minded soul may be rescued ere the giant has devoured him; some captive spirit delivered from the snare of the destroyer.

Mr. Feeble-mind.—The nature of the Giant may, perhaps, best be learned by studying the character of his victim. His own account of himself is very touching and beautiful, and withal instructive too. It supplies another phase of spiritual experience, and somewhat resembles the character of LITTLE-FAITH of the former Part, and that of MR. FEARING and others in the present narrative.

This man was brought to serious thought about his soul by the frequent reminders he received daily that he was not to live always here. This induced him to undertake the pilgrimage. He was, however, one of those who are the victims of constitutional weakness and infirmity of spirit. Such sickly Pilgrims need many of the comforts and consolations of the Spirit, and, in God's mercy, they receive them. But for the daily intervention of special providences in their favor, they would utterly fail; and yet, even with these special helps, they are liable to assault and likely to be overcome. The one thing in this poor man's favor was, that his heart went not before him into temptation; the root of the matter was still within him; it was his weakness, not his will, that caused him to yield to the giant's power. And, seeing that his heart was still fixed on heavenly things, God had mercy upon him, and delivered him out of all his afflictions; and now attaches him to a Pilgrim-band with whom he may be more safe, and, in the sympathy of their strength, may yet become more strong.

Mr. Not-right struck dead.—This man was wholly wrong, hopelessly lost. Therefore, being bad, he is far from the power of SLAY-GOOD, and thus escapes only to fall a victim to a severer stroke of judgment. Of the two, the Giant would rather have FEEBLE-MIND, for he was on his journey to the King, while NOT-RIGHT was on the highway to the Giant's master, caught already as his certain prey.

Matthew and Mercy married.—A double marriage takes place here—MATTHEW is married to MERCY; and PHEBE, the daughter of GAIUS, is married to JAMES. These marriages are undoubtedly "in the Lord." When pilgrims thus intermarry, they prove mutually helpful in the way of the pilgrimage.

Pay from the Good Samaritan.—This is a beautiful allusion to the parable of our Lord, and shows that if GAIUS "kept an inn" for the refreshment of pilgrims, it was not for purposes of worldly gain, and that the entertainment there was purely of a spiritual character. It is a comforting thought to the wayfarers of the road that they are spiritually cared for and supported at the King's charges; that their supply of "daily bread" comes from his bountiful hand; and that by his care they are brought on their way to the Better Land. So they purpose to proceed upon their journey.

Feeble-mind intended to linger.—How touching is this story of poor FEEBLE-MIND! Although he is in this brave company, yet he feels worse than if he were alone. He is so weak, and they are so strong, he cannot but feel a want of sympathy with his own state and experience. He is a type of that class of Christian men who are of weak and tender conscience, easily offended, and made weak. The Christian liberty of other men stumbles him. He therefore feels that he may prove but a burden to his fellow-pilgrims, and longs for some companion of like spirit with his own, with whom he might keep easy pace in the path of the pilgrimage.

But see how GREAT-HEART deals with his weak brother! This bold, brave, lion-hearted man stoops to the necessities of his feebleminded comrade; and, in his answer, he gives expression to the very spirit of the Gospel of the grace of God. In a body constituted as is the Church of Christ on earth, there are diversities of character: some are weak and some are strong. Now, plainly, the strong must have some duty to perform towards those that are weak. St. Paul provides for this— He tells us that conscience must be the judge for each man's conduct. But if there should come a conflict of consciences—the strong and the weak—what then? Is the strong man's conscience, by reason of its strength, to overbear the conscience of the weak? No; rather must the strong man's conscience yield to the conscience of the weak, lest a stumbling-block be cast in the way of a weak brother for whom Christ hath died. GREAT-HEART has learned this great principle of the Gospel;

and, accordingly, he pronounces himself ready to stoop very low, and to resign many things, and to exercise great forbearance of his Christian liberty, rather than this man should be left behind, or be caused, by his example, to stumble in the way. We have all much to learn from this exercise of the Christian liberty of GREAT-HEART, the brave conductor of the pilgrimage.

Ready-to-halt came by.—Notwithstanding GREAT-HEART'S willingness to conform in all things to MR. FEEBLE-MIND'S necessities, yet God's mercy grants the wish of the feeble Pilgrim; and, lo! as they are debating, one came by, whose name is READY-TO-HALT. This man leans upon crutches; and, though weak, is yet consistently pursuing his pilgrimage.

In a side-note, Bunyan interprets the "crutches" to mean "the Promises," upon which this halting Christian has learned to lean and to support himself. Here, then, is a companion who will walk with FEEBLE-MIND, and enter into the feeling of his infirmities, and thoroughly sympathize with him in his lowly state and condition. And both these men, naturally and constitutionally feeble and halting, will be made strong, and be brought on their way by the friendly aid and Christian forbearance of their stronger companions, who have meekly learned the great Gospel duty—"To the weak became I as weak, that I might gain the weak: I am made all things to all men, that I might by all means save some," 1 Corinthians 9:22.

PART II.
CHAPTER IX.

VANITY FAIR AND MR. MNASON'S HOUSE.

INTRODUCTION.—Onward still moves the company of the Second Pilgrimage; and now, without hurt or damage, without any serious downfall or drawback, they approach, under the brave conduct of their guide, to the vicinity of Vanity Fair.

Our minds instinctively turn back upon the memories of the former visit to this stage of the journey. We have, indeed, been expecting to be again introduced to the self-same scenes, seeing, as it is said in the former Part, that "the way to the Celestial City lies just through the town where this lusty fair is kept." But how altered is it now! It is, indeed, the same bad, wicked place, loving the same vanities, devoted to the same pleasures, bent upon the same pursuits. But "the offence of the Cross" has comparatively ceased. The seed planted by the protest of the former Pilgrims has already borne fruit. Persecutions for the faith are now unknown; a remnant of its people is reserved for the Lord; and the communion of saints may be enjoyed even within the precincts of Vanity Fair!

As in the preceding stage of Christian communion, so in this, Bunyan borrows the name of the host from among those early Christians who are immortalized in sacred story as having been "given to hospitality." There once went a pilgrim-band, with the great Apostle of the Gentiles at its head, bound for Jerusalem, of which it is said, "There went with us also certain of the disciples of Caesarea, and brought with them one MNASON of Cyprus, an old disciple, with whom we should lodge," Acts 21:16. The name of this man is now very appropriately introduced into the narrative, indicating the person to whom the Pilgrims are indebted for "harbor and good company," during their stay and sojourn in Vanity Fair.

They consulted with one another.—The Pilgrims are nearing a point of danger—danger hitherto attaching to both body and soul. In anticipation of possible perils, they take counsel together. They have the fate of FAITHFUL and the experience of CHRISTIAN before their eyes; and it needs some forethought and preparation before they commit themselves to like protests and perils of the town of Vanity. On the eve of some great battle, a council of war is held; in prospect of some vast expedition, the projectors take mutual counsel and advice. So, in advance of spiritual dangers and tests, it behooves the wayfaring Pilgrims to advise with each other in godly and spiritual consultation.

One Mnason, a Cyprusian.—How comfortable to know that in this godless town there is a home for the Christian, a communion-place for Pilgrims, an altar erected to the Lord of all! There was a time when former Pilgrims found in it no home, no friend, no sweet communion of faithful men. In those days there was but rage, and hatred, and ungoverned fury against the servants of the Lord; a partial jury, a prejudiced judge, perjured witnesses, and persecution as the punishment of those that loved the truth. But now there is a seed to serve the Lord. God-fearing men and Christ-loving men are permitted to live within its bounds. A congregation of faithful men is gathered from among its population, and godly communion and fellowship may be largely and blessedly enjoyed there.

Outside of the town.—The little flock must be separate, as Israel in Goshen, not dwelling among the Egyptians. Within the walls some possibly may live, and all may be obliged to conduct their ordinary business; but for spiritual purposes they must be apart and away from the crowd and bustle of a place so wholly given to Mammon as the town of Vanity. We must learn to withdraw ourselves into the peace and quietude of Christian fellowship; and there, apart from the busy haunts of men, and away from the distracting occupations of our own lives, to hold communion with our God and Savior, and with the people of his choice.

Harbor and good company.—The wants of pilgrims here below may be summed up in these two requirements—a place of safety to abide in, and the company of like-minded men to communicate with, whereby spiritual supplies are poured into the heart, and the Pilgrim-band is fed and furnished for the perils and necessities of the outward way.

More particularly in such a place as Vanity is it pleasant to meet with spiritual fare and friends. The latter, however, are but few, but yet are as the moon and stars at night. We may not have full sunshine; but, at least, amid the darkness of this dark world, God reveals the moonlight radiance and the star-light gems—the reflected glories of the Sun of Righteousness. The light in which the

Christian walks in this world is as the light of the moon—sometimes waxing, sometimes waning. Fellow-Christians are as welcome to our path as are the bright stars in the firmament to the weary traveler at nightfall. Christian men, like stars, receive light and reflect light; thus shedding their bright but borrowed rays down upon the dark pavement of human society—

> "Nor let the meanest think
> His lamp too dim;
> In this dark world
> The Lord hath need of him."*

Some notable rubs.—The Pilgrims compare notes and exchange their experiences of the way. Old HONEST and Mr. GREAT-HEART detail some of the salient points of the pilgrimage; and then the whole party are counseled by the good and timely advice of these good men, who have been gathered out of the giddy multitude of Vanity into the congregation of Christ's flock. The names of these men are suggestive of the feelings and experiences of those who have been delivered from the sins of Vanity, and yet must dwell in the midst of this naughty world.

CONTRITE is impressed with deep sorrow for sin past, and, true to his nature, enjoins watchfulness against the rising seeds of indwelling sin. HOLY-MAN would have us to be separate from sinners; and, for this purpose, to possess the characteristics of godly courage and true holiness—requirements essentially needed in a world of sin and strong temptation. LOVE-SAINTS knows the value of Christian fellowship; and, seeing how few the little flock ever are, he loves them each, he loves them all. Though the flock be small, yet it would be very strong if bound and banded together in the spirit of love, which is "the very bond of peace and of all virtues." DARE-NOT-LIE abhors the falsehoods and deceitful ways of the world, and would incorporate into the Christian body the character of truth and truthfulness. Lies and deceptions are the rags and rents of the Pilgrim's garb—the incongruities of the Pilgrim's rule and raiment. The Christian wears "the girdle of truth about his loins." Lastly, PENITENT has ever the remembrance of his sin before his face, and grieves that he should have so grievously offended his Lord, and fears to offend again.

Here the group is again augmented by another double marriage. Their host bestows his two daughters in marriage to CHRISTIANA'S

---
*James Montgomery, "Occupy Till I Come."

remaining sons, giving GRACE to SAMUEL, and MARTHA to JOSEPH. These marriages are also "in the Lord," believers equally yoked together, making up a company of Christians, members of one family, large in faith, and abounding in good works; wielding a Christian influence, and making it felt, in their locality and neighborhood. Would that it were so with all the Christian families of the land!

A monster out of the woods.—This evidently is an historical allusion, and seems to refer particularly to the spread of the power of the Papacy for some time before the period of the Revolution in 1688, whereby many were drawn into the net of superstition, and children were educated in the tenets and doctrines of the Church of Rome. This danger was met by able men of the period, men who loved the truth, and uttered a bold and manly protest against error. Some of the ablest controversial essays against the distinctive doctrines of the Roman Catholic Church were issued during that period, including the "Morning Exercises," delivered at Cripplegate, and the series of tracts or essays afterwards compiled by Dr. Gibson, Bishop of London, and recently re-issued in a series of volumes entitled "Gibson's Preservative against Popery." The writers of these works, no doubt, were the GREAT-HEARTS and HONESTS of the day, who went forth to subdue the spirit of the wrathful and destructive monster of the woods.

PART II.
CHAPTER X.

THE DELECTABLE MOUNTAINS AND THE SHEPHERDS.

INTRODUCTION.—This chapter contains a record of some bold and manly exploits of the Pilgrim-band. Their numbers are many, and their faith is strong; and therefore they feel disposed to leave their foot-prints on the way, not way-marks of weakness, but permanent records of their strength and Christian prowess. The experiments of believing faith are always bold ventures, designed for the removal of some wrong, or the prevention of some evil, or the establishment of some good thing—to be in after-times a help and assistance to other Pilgrims who may pass that way. Accordingly, the lot of the Pilgrims having just now fallen in pleasant places, they are invigorated for the march; and, as the result of the large provision and refreshment they have received, they propose a very manly and Christian undertaking—the destruction of Doubting Castle and its great master, Giant DESPAIR. Here there is great play allowed to the diverse characters of the company—the strong men fighting, and the weak ones tarrying among the baggage, showing that there is work for each and for all, not only in the Lord's vineyard, but also in the Lord's battle-field.

The account of the interview with the Shepherds in the Second Pilgrimage falls short of the former narrative, both in depth of sentiment and in vigor of conception. It is less simple, and therefore less sublime. It fails to note any prospect of the Celestial City as having been seen through the telescope. Perhaps CHRISTIANA and her companions were so strong in faith and so constant in hope as not to need this additional evidence, which was granted to CHRISTIAN and HOPEFUL as a compensation for their sorrows of despair, and to comfort them while their hands yet trembled from the fearful sights they had seen from the Mount of Error and the Hill of Caution. But, surely, it would have been a stroke worthy of Bunyan's pen to have pictured FEEBLE-MIND and READY-TO-HALT permitted to see the golden gates of the City. Such a sight of far-seeing faith would perhaps have enabled the former to put away his "fears," and the latter to cast away his "crutches," and no longer, as weak Pilgrims, *to fall back upon* the promises as an external help, but, as strong men, to journey on *in the inward strength* of the promises of God, and in the sure faith of his Word. But feeble and halting Pilgrims never do see very distant prospects. Their faith is too faint for that; and yet at last they enter into rest.

They came to the river.—This is "the river of the water of life," beside whose streams the former Pilgrims had for a season enjoyed such quietude and rest. To the present company also this "river of God" is pleasant and refreshing; its evergreens cover the Pilgrims with their peaceful shade; and they can lie down, and sleep, and be in safety. There is further added to the scene, as here described, the tender care bestowed by our good heavenly Father upon the little ones of his flock. This allusion is suggested by the circumstances of the Pilgrims—children having been born to those God-fearing couples who have, as narrated in the preceding scenes, been married in the Lord. Here, then, are their children cared for and tended by the loving Lord of the hill; and provision is made both to "feed the sheep" and to "feed the lambs" of the flock. "So," says Bunyan, "they were content to commit their little ones to him."

By-path meadow, to the stile.—How different are the thoughts of different men at the same point of the Pilgrimage! We recall to mind the conversation of CHRISTIAN and HOPEFUL, when, in the moment of temptation, they sought to avoid the flints of the way by turning aside into the soft meadow-path. But now a very different consultation is being held at this same stile: the Pilgrims are in high deliberation not only how to avoid the danger for themselves, but more especially how to destroy it for the sake of others. The former Pilgrims went by this stile only to fall into the grasp of the Giant's power; these Pilgrims go forth from this stile to lay the Giant in the unyielding grasp of Death, and to lay his castle even with the ground.

If it were lawful to go.—The propriety of making such bold ventures on the enemy's ground is sometimes questionable. Some men are not strong enough to resist Despair, much less would they be strong enough to destroy him. It is dangerous to trifle with so bold an undertaking. Unless the plain and unmistakable voice of duty calls, it is better to pass on. The physician may walk the hospital; this is his vocation and calling: but if you desire to escape infection, it will be advisable to keep aloof from danger. With some, yea, with many Christians, it would only be that instead of overcoming Despair, they would themselves be destroyed of the destroyer.

But GREAT-HEART has a great commission to fulfill, and has strength of faith commensurate with his calling. *He* can boldly fight this good fight; and whosoever goes forth with him, depending on the same strength, will also overcome. Accordingly, in this party a discrimination is made. Only the strong, the brave, the mighty men of valor may undertake the conflict; the weak, the feeble-minded, the faint-hearted must stay behind, and not adventure themselves into so perilous a strife.

So they went up.—It is easy to awake the Giant, and easy to provoke him; but he must be a brave man that can go up against him and defy him. And even the bravest hero of the army of Christ will do well not to assail him single-handed, but rather in company. Despair is that dark foe that assaults men's consciences, and, through doubts and fears, brings them into captivity. Whoso, by putting forth a strong hand, destroys Despair, performs a deed that is worthy of everlasting remembrance.

And in the destruction of this great Giant, souls are sure to be delivered. Many have lain in his dungeons unrelieved by any aid from Christian brethren; but never have Christian men put forth a faithful effort in this direction, but they have opened the door to some beleaguered captive. CHRISTIAN and HOPEFUL, it is true, were delivered by the Key of Promise from within; but DESPONDENCY and MUCH-AFRAID were delivered by the assault of GREAT-HEART from without. "There are diversities of operations."*

The Delectable Mountains.—All that has been written in the former Allegory respecting these mountains and the shepherds that had their flocks there, is fully borne out by the details of this second visit; with this additional characteristic—that they receive and welcome the weak as well as the strong. Like the Great Shepherd, so do these under-shepherds of the flock: they carry the weak ones on their shoulders, and the little ones in their bosom. Their tidings of welcome, their sympathizing words, their soothing invitations, are for the tender and sensitive ones, who, but for this kindly dealing, might not have sufficient boldness to come. These shepherds are the pastors of the flock, the ministers of the Word.

Mount Marvel.—The man of mighty faith who is seen from hence

---

*1 Corinthians 12:6—And there are diversities of operations, but it is the same God which worketh all in all.

is said to be the son of GREAT-GRACE. Worthy son of such a father! GREAT-GRACE had power to affright the thieves and to disperse the bandits of the way. Were it but the sound of his chariot wheels, or the prancing of his horses' hoofs that is heard upon the road, the way is cleared, for GREAT-GRACE is at hand. And if the father could disperse robbers, the son can remove mountains. Here the power of living faith is magnified and made honorable.

Mount Innocence.—"To keep himself unspotted from the world" is one of the marks of the man who is possessed of true and undefiled religion, James 1:27. Pure innocence, unless it contaminate itself, cannot be defiled. The mire of the streets clings not to the robe of innocence. If ever it lose its luster or defile its purity, it is its own fault, by walking in unclean places and contracting guilt.

Mount Charity.—True charity "never faileth." It is that which ever gives, and ever receives, and never exhausts its supply. It is a perennial stream, watering others, and itself continually supplied from above. It is as the widow's cruse of oil—its last remnant granted to the prophet becomes a never-failing supply, increased by the prophet's Lord.

FOOL *and one* WANT-WIT.—External washings take no effect upon the inward corruption, but to make it more corrupt, adding the sin of hypocrisy to other sins. The Pharisees were accounted more sinful than others, because they were more pretentious and more boastful, Matthew 5:20; Luke 18:14.

Mercy and the looking-glass.—This is one of the most instructive of the emblems of the present stage. MERCY longs for a certain looking-glass; her desire is satisfied, and she discovers the peculiar character and power of this mirror: in it a man may first see himself, and afterwards may see the Savior. This is a very beautiful allusion to two very remarkable passages of Scripture—James 1:23-25, and 2 Corinthians 3:18.

This mirror is the Word of God. The Bible is the Christian's looking-glass, in which he is to see, and read, and observe, and know himself. It is a true mirror, and presents us to ourselves as we really are. It speaks the truth, and flatters not. A blessing is pronounced upon the man that looks therein and "continues" to look, James 1:25. What is this "blessing" thus promised to him that continues to behold himself in the mirror of the Word? It is this: that he will behold two visions—(1) He sees the sinner in himself, what he is; and (2), he sees the sinner in Christ, what he may become. Only "continue" in the study of this true mirror; for never yet did a man read the Bible long without being rewarded with the view of Christ his Savior. There is more about Christ in the Bible than about yourself; and the next thing to the view of the degradation of the sinner is the view of the glory of the Savior.

This is the spiritual dissolving-view which is thus presented in the Christian mirror—"But we all, with open face beholding *as in a glass* the glory of the Lord, are *changed* into the same image from glory to glory, even as by the Spirit of the Lord," 2 Corinthians 3:18. We remember HOPEFUL'S earnest prayer—"Father, reveal thy Son!" And in the conversation on the Enchanted Ground, this good man thus remarks—"Christ is so hid in God from the natural apprehension of the flesh, that he cannot by any man be savingly known, unless God the Father reveals Him to him." And in the mirror of the Word, "the law of liberty," he *is* revealed.

Thus (1) "the Christian's looking-glass," as a law of bondage, reveals us to ourselves in all our sin, defilement, and corruption; and then (2) as "the law of liberty," the view of self is "changed" into the likeness of the Savior.

In the next chapter we shall see the consequences of sin in the admonitory details given as respecting the character of "Turnaway." Once his face was Sion-ward; but he turned back, and would walk no more in that way. Tired of toiling up the steep ascent, he suddenly resigned himself to the downward path. He now began to hate the things he once did love. The sight of the most affecting scenes of the Savior's love only tended the more to embitter his soul, and to renew his desperate resolution. Ministers of the Word would reason with him, and pray with him, and lay their sympathizing hands upon him; but all in vain.

PART II.
CHAPTER XI.

MR. VALIANT-FOR-TRUTH.

INTRODUCTION.—Christian valor, influenced and impelled by Christian doctrine, is the principle inculcated in the person of VALIANT-FOR-TRUTH, whose strife and conflict, consistency and faith, are here set forth as an illustration of the power of Divine grace, and as an example to all who, receiving like faith and precious promises, would fight the good fight, endure to the end, and finish their course with joy.

The sketch of this man's career is possessed of a twofold value: it illustrates (1) the power of resistance which belongs to true faith; and (2) the character of the opposition that assails the truth, and would turn aside the Pilgrim, by fears and forebodings of speculative perils. The Allegory would be incomplete without this specimen of Christian character, holding its own, and steadily pursuing its course, notwithstanding the hosts of unbelief and speculation that gathered themselves together to check its ardor and to intercept its progress. Here we have a true Pilgrim, who in his own person stands the brunt of nearly all the oppositions and antagonisms of both Pilgrimages—not, indeed, in actual encounter, but in the gloomy anticipations and dark surmisings of fearful, or fanciful, or faithless friends. How many fears are conjured up; how many foes are pictured to the carnal eye; how many fancies and imaginative perils are summoned to the fight; how many truths are distorted into lies, facts tortured into the service of prejudice, successes quoted as reverses; and, after all, the carnal wish is found to be the father to the carnal thought!

This kind of danger being thus indicated, the antidote is also largely illustrated in the character and conduct of Mr. VALIANT-FOR-TRUTH. His one answer throughout is—TELL-TRUE has told me one thing; other persons tell me the very opposite; I will believe what TELL-TRUE says. This is true faith, and the abiding consistency of faith. This man has found the rock, and builds upon it. Thus the surging floods of opposition rise, the impetuous rains of unbelief descend, the rending storms of desperation blow, and all these opposing elements "beat vehemently upon that house, and cannot shake it; for it is founded upon a rock," Luke 6:48.

Valiant-for-truth.—The hero of this scene of the PROGRESS is now presented to our view in the person of this bold and steadfast man. This point of the road is dangerous, haunted by robbers and bandits. Here LITTLE-FAITH had suffered loss. But now a braver and more valiant Pilgrim is encountered, who knows his strength and the source of his strength. He has fought a lengthened conflict, and, his assailants being put to flight, he is found by GREAT-HEART standing in the road-way, sword in hand, with the marks of sore combat—wounds and blood.

From the names given to these assailants, it would appear that this assault was not of the same character as that of LITTLE-FAITH. The Pilgrim of the former narrative had encountered spiritual enemies from within—FAINT-HEART, MISTRUST, and GUILT; while this Pilgrim seems to have been assailed by carnal enemies from without, as indicated by their names—WILD-HEAD, INCONSIDERATE, and PRAGMATIC. Mr. Scott observes—"The author meant to represent by them certain *wild* enthusiasts who, not having ever duly *considered* any religious subject, *officiously* intrude themselves in the way of professors, to perplex their minds and persuade them that, unless they adopt their reveries or superstitions, they cannot be saved."

The conflict, however, was a severe one. It was fought against great odds (humanly speaking), and victory inclined to the side of faith and truth. 1. He fought in the strength of his King, whom he implored to send him aid and succor. 2. He fought with the proper weapon, the true-tempered sword of the Spirit, quick, and sharper than any two-edged sword. 3. And he wielded this sword with skill and constancy. Hence his undoubted victory. He now joins the Pilgrim-company, and forms another addition to the group; an addition, too, that promises to make the band more strong and steadfast to bear the concluding stages of the journey.

He questioned with him.—The narrative of this man, as elicited in course of conversation, reveals a remarkable ordeal of Christian consistency in running the race. He had come out of darkness—Dark-land was his native home. Into this dark place the light had shined in the visit of TELL-TRUE. Here is the message of God, by the hand of one of his servants, pouring a flood of light upon at least one dark heart. The experiences of CHRISTIAN and his pilgrimage were the means of attracting the man's affections towards the Narrow-way. Thus the spiritual biography of one man may become the prolific seed of many new-born souls. This citizen of Dark-land received the light, and believed the tidings; for both light and tidings were revealed by TELL-TRUE.

And now, see the ordeal of test and trial through which this newly enlightened convert is called to pass. He alone has received the light; all else is dark in Dark-land. Even within his own home he meets, not with sympathy, but with opposition—all the harder to resist, seeing it proceeded from those whom he was bound to obey in all necessary matters of filial duly.

Here the conflict begins—with hints and innuendos, with misrepresentations of the path, and exaggerations of its danger, and with all sorts of objections—the result of either ignorance, or prejudice, or malice—in order, if possible, to deter the young man from undertaking the pilgrimage. The most is made of the difficulties of the way, and stress is laid upon the mis-adventures of false pilgrims. The lions and giants of course, form a frightful scene in their picture, and the darkness of the Shadow of Death is spoken of as though the inhabitants of Dark-land had never seen anything but light! Not content with exaggerating the actual dangers, they proceed to falsify the true experiences of the way. They overlook CHRISTIAN'S triumphs; indeed, they report them as sad reverses; and thus they combined to bring up an evil report of the land.

And is this foreign to our own experience of the way of the world and worldly men in their dealing with the cause of religion? Do they not accuse that way wrongfully, and lay to its charge things that belong not to it? The profession of religion involves trouble and loss; the possession of religion calls for self-denial and the bearing of many a cross. Well, instantly the way is spoken against, and young believers are discouraged. Or professors fail and turn aside; unworthy pilgrims intrude upon the King's highway, and come to an ill end. All this is laid to the account of true religion; and the world seeks to scandalize the faith for the fault of its professors. Such were the hindrances which obstructed the pilgrimage of Mr. VALIANT-FOR-TRUTH.

I believed Tell-true.—This was the secret of his confidence and constancy. Men told him of drawbacks, and downfalls, and pits, and snares, and lions, and giants, and dungeons, and dark rivers, and death-pains; but none of these things moved him. He had heard from the lips of Tell-true that Christian forsook all and followed Christ, and, through the trials and crosses of the homeward journey, he reached Home at last. He *believed* this; his faith impelled him to the pilgrimage, and hitherto had the Lord helped him.

PART II.
CHAPTER XII.

THE ENCHANTED GROUND.

INTRODUCTION.—Three important scenes and lessons occur in this chapter, which contains the account of the passage of the Pilgrims through the Enchanted Ground—(1) The danger of the Pilgrim-band, and their earnest struggles to resist the perils that encompassed them; (2) the deadly peril of other Pilgrims, who, contrary to all the safe directions given him, had fallen asleep, and could not be awaked; and (3) the introduction of one STAND-FAST to the group, and the additional profit and instruction contributed to the Allegory by his spiritual experience.

The Enchanted Ground wears a darker and more dangerous aspect in this Pilgrimage than in the former narrative. CHRISTIAN and HOPEFUL had found their chief enemy there to be their spirit of drowsiness and inclination to sleep. But, admonished by the advice of the Shepherds, they sustained each other by godly fellowship and interchange of their mutual experience. In this Pilgrimage the perils of the journey are additionally enhanced by the darkness and by the general badness of the way, involving slips and downfalls. But their company is strong—GREAT-HEART in the forefront, and VALIANT-FOR-TRUTH in the rereward, and all the rest between; a beautiful illustration of the adjustment of different talents and the equilibrium of spiritual strength and weakness that must ever characterize a well-ordered company of spiritual Pilgrims.

The character of STAND-FAST is beautifully introduced, and is well wrought out, even to the close. He is a wrestling Christian, striving against sin, and doing battle "on his knees" against the carnal temptations of the world and the flesh. We have stated in the notes of the former Pilgrimage that the Enchanted Ground is meant to indicate a state of temporal prosperity, in which men are inclined to slumber, and ease, and luxurious indulgence of the flesh. And, accordingly, this is the very temptation that assails STAND-FAST in this perilous place. Madam BUBBLE is the ably-drawn picture of the present evil world, in its manifold and strong temptation of the fleshly nature and of the carnal sense. And after a man has gained the world and lost his soul, what has he gained?—a bubble! what has he lost?—his life, eternity, and all!

The Enchanted Ground.—The natural tendency of this place is to make one drowsy. The enchantments of the world are dangerous to the spiritual health, tending to stupefy the soul, and to bring it into the captivity of spiritual lethargy and unconcern. It represents that state of carnal ease and worldly prosperity that rocks the spiritual man to slumber, bewitching him with the world's smiles and sunshine, and causing him to forget God. The stumblings and downfalls of the Pilgrims indicate the dangers of such a state of spiritual night and darkness; and the arbor, with its soft and tender couch, means the utter relapse of the soul, entirely resigned to the pleasures of life, and spell-bound by its wily enchantments.

The mist and darkness of this stage are consistent with the spirit of the enchanted scene. Worldly pleasure waves her magic wand, and bids a cloud of misty incense to arise, and mysterious darkness to descend; and under these influences the soul is induced to slumber and to sleep the deep slumber, it may be, the deadly sleep of oblivion and forgetfulness. The soul needs light in such a place, and by that light the Pilgrims do well to read the directions of the way, lest they too should be entangled in "the net of the flatterer," or in some other yoke of bondage.

There is also great danger here lest we mistake the true nature of the right way. In days of ease and worldly peace we are liable to choose "the cleanest way," and to avoid the narrow path because it may, for the time, *seem* to be less pleasant to the tread. Here it is important, yea, essential, that we consult a map, seeing that by this only can we tell whither each way leads, and what is the end to which each path conducts. This is the place wherein to walk with wary steps and wakeful eye—"by faith, and not by sight."

Heedless and Too-bold.—These men are described as having thus far advanced upon their journey; but now, at one of the later stages, they are overpowered, not by any direct assault of Satan, but by the soft and indulgent spirit of slumber. Here Satan's power is strong, and all the more insidious because it is unseen. It steals softly over the soul, and sheds the soporific dew upon the eyelids of the understanding, making us heavy with sleep and weary of the way. It is Satan's last hour and the power of darkness. So near the Land of

Beulah and yet asleep! but a single stage removed from the end of the journey—"almost," but not "altogether" saved!—Acts 26:28–29. As Bunyan elsewhere speaks of King Agrippa—"He stepped fair, but stepped short. He was hot while he ran, but he was quickly out of breath." This is a timely admonition to us all, even to those that are farthest traveled on the road, that we be watchful to the end, and so much the more as we see the day approaching.

They cried out.—In prayer, as CHRISTIAN had done in his days of darkness, and as all true Pilgrims must do, if they would walk safely through the dim shadows that obscure the evidence of the soul. In all time of our wealth, and in all seasons of pleasure and prosperity, we have as much need of the weapon of All-prayer as in the dark days of adversity. Darkness gathers around the soul amid the enchantments of the Enchanted Ground, as well as amid the spirits of the vast deep in the Valley of the Shadow of Death.

One that was much concerned.—The intensity of the danger, and the extreme necessity of the Pilgrims at this stage, are well described by this scene of the praying Pilgrim, STAND-FAST. "Behold, he prayeth!" What darkness hath befallen him; what danger threatened him; what sore affliction is it that hath thus brought him to his knees? STAND-FAST, no doubt, has borne many a brunt of battle, and in days of open danger has been caparisoned for the fight, and has fought his battles bravely. But he is now walking amid the enchantments of earthly scenes; and, lo, an enchantress stands beside him to allure him from the path of safety. In this time of danger the tempted Pilgrim betakes himself to prayer.

Madam Bubble.—Here is the world, with its chief enchantments, tempting what remains of the carnal sense and of the fleshly mind, so as to wake up its last surviving spark of earthliness, and lull the "new man" into its deadly sleep—

"Till the swollen bubble bursts—and all is air!"

This phantom world, this painted parti-colored bubble, that men covet, and chase, and cherish, and for which most men sell their very souls—this earthly element now strives to tempt the Pilgrim. This is the Delilah of the pilgrimage—the enchantress of the Enchanted Ground. If thou wilt but lay thy head upon her lap, and rest thee, while she lulls thee into sleep, all thy days are henceforth days of weakness, blindness, and captivity. Had the strong Samson knelt in prayer in the day of the Philistines, *he* had been STAND-FAST to the end. But he slept as many sleep; on the Enchanted Ground, and all was lost!

Then I took me to my knees.—This was his safety. In any other strength than this he could but fail. Hence prayer is always needed; for this temptation ever assails us. So long as we are in the world, the spirit of the world would woo and win us, to the loss of our eternal gain. Beware of Madam BUBBLE, all ye Pilgrims who would be safe. She follows to the final stages, even to the brink of the river does she tempt you. Then pray all through the pilgrimage. Be not fascinated by her wiles, nor yet enchanted by her spells. Betake you to your knees in prayer, that ye may be "able to withstand in the evil day, and having done all, to stand," Ephesians 6:13.

The same character of danger that assailed FAITHFUL at the outset of his journey in the carnal temptation of ADAM THE FIRST, now assails STAND-FAST near the end of his pilgrimage. The world, and the spirit of the world, would entangle us in the wilderness, and make a truce with us, and so hinder the progress of our journey home. It is for us to resist her enchantments and reject her overtures. "What peace, so long as her witchcrafts are so many?" 2 Kings 9:22.

> "I, under fair pretence of friendly ends,
> And well-placed words of glozing courtesy,
> Baited with reasons not unplausible,
> Wind me into the easy-hearted man,
> And hug him into snares."*

---

*John Milton, "Comus."

PART II.
CHAPTER XIII.

THE PILGRIMS AT HOME.

INTRODUCTION.—We have arrived at the conclusion of the Second Pilgrimage—the last stage, the farewell to the things of earth, the welcome to the world of light and everlasting life. There is a sublimity in the description of these final scenes which excels that of the former Part. The group that has been gradually enlarging is now about to break up and to dissolve into the Invisible. In the portraiture of this concluding stage, the Dreamer summons to his aid all his powers of imagery and description. A perspective opens upon the view—a continuous series of scenes, as the Pilgrim-band breaks up, piecemeal, one by one. Gathered together in the Land of Beulah, they peacefully await the summons of their Lord. They pass not the fords of the river in company, as CHRISTIAN and HOPEFUL did, but singly, and each alone. In the description of these successive departures, there is included all the solemnity of earthly solicitude with all the heavenly bliss and peace characteristic of the death-bed scene of the departing Christian.

This gorgeous sketch, thus pictured in detail, is well worth the study and review of the thoughtful and pious mind. Post after post arrives with the summons of the Lord, borne on the arrow tipped with death, yet fraught with everlasting life. Link after link of this wondrous chain is severed, and soul after soul bids fond adieu to earth, and is helped across the flood to the further shore. Here all is changed: the weak are changed from weakness into strength; the desponding, from gloom and sorrow into joy; the strong and happy, from glory into glory. CHRISTIANA, as a mother in Israel, is first called away, and leaves kind messages of love to all her fellow-pilgrims; and then departs to be with CHRISTIAN and with CHRISTIAN'S Lord. READY-TO-HALT, out of weakness, is made strong, and enters into the realization of the Promises. FEEBLE-MIND girds up the loins of his mind, and passes to the other side. DESPONDENCY and his daughter fear and despond no more; their earthly murmurs break forth into songs and melodies of heaven. Mr. HONEST has to dare the deeper fords and to cross the overflowings of the river; and, by the help of GOOD-CONSCIENCE, is conducted safely through the flood. VALIANT-FOR-TRUTH sinks low in deep waters, but rises to the higher victory. And STAND-FAST, although "the waters are to the palate bitter, and to the stomach cold," yet has he no fears, but stands fast and firm even to the end, and at length "ceased to be seen of them." Thus did these members of the Pilgrim-band dissolve in death, to meet again and for ever on the better and brighter shore of the Spirit-land.

The Land of Beulah.—The border-land of heaven is Beulah—that spiritual state of peace and rest, in which God ever comforts his children, and feeds them with heavenly food, and visits them with his grace and love, and departs not from the holy place of the heart within which Jesus is enshrined as the loved and chosen guest. "Thou shalt be called Hephzibah, and thy land Beulah: for the Lord delighteth in thee; and thy land shall be married," Isaiah 62:4. This is the place of the espousal of the soul to Jesus—

> "The Bride and bridegroom both rejoice
> In Beulah's marriage scene;
> While earth and heaven unite their voice,
> And Jordan rolls between."

All the Pilgrim-band are resting here, as they alone can rest who abide in Jesus and are stayed upon his love. They are now hard by the waters of Death, and are ripening fast for the reaper's sickle. Amid the pleasures of his grace and the consolations of his love, they await the message bearing the summons of their Lord.

There was a post come.—And now the company is about to break up, and CHRISTIANA is the first to go. Death is the messenger of God to man to take him home. It comes on the arrow-point; sharp and painful it may be, but it is an arrow of love. It breaks the cord of this mortal life, but only to bind it again, in an indissoluble bond, to the heart of Jesus.

Such a one as CHRISTIANA has many things to say, many messages to leave, many adieus to present to those that have borne her company in the way. To each she speaks, according to his want, according to his weakness, or according to his strength. She sets her house in order, commits her children and children's children to the good offices of strong and valiant men, comforts all her fellows with the consolation wherewith she also is comforted, and now is ready to depart and be with Christ—for ever with the Lord.

And what a death-bed is that of the full-ripe Christian! Both shores are filled with the communion of saints, while the river flows between. On earth they throng around her bed-side, and stand as it were along the sloping strand by the river-brink. In heaven a yet more glorious throng awaits her—of chariots and horses, and white-robed priests and kings, to lift her from the fast-flowing tide, and upbear her to the golden gates and to the all-glorious throne. And this scene is ended!

Mr. Ready-to-halt.—And now this lame and limping Pilgrim is summoned. He has leaned upon his crutches hitherto; but now the chariots of the Lord await him. They that trust God's promises, and lean upon his Word, shall have the full enjoyment of them all in the land where there is no more hope or promise, for all is the full fruition of eternal glory. We take not the promises with us into heaven, but leave them behind us for other Pilgrims of the way.

Mr. Feeble-mind.—The former victim of Giant SLAY-GOOD is now summoned to his rest. In feebleness he had trod the path; he had gone softly all his days; but withal he had been faithful to his King. For this he is rewarded at the last, and, as a sickly, weakly child, is taken to his great Father's bosom. In deep humility he had walked, in very humiliation he ever loved to live; his death-bed was a lowly cot; and no better burying-place does he desire than "the dung-hill." To this humble-minded man is now the message sent—"Friend, come up higher!" He invokes "faith and patience" to abide with him to the last, and passes to the other side.

Despondency and Much-afraid.—Born of the same blood, characterized by the same spirit, bound once in the same bondage of Doubting Castle, "in death they were not divided." And in putting off this mortality and the fleshly raiment, they put off also their doubts and fears. The seeds of doubt had lingered to the last. The iron of despair had entered into their soul, and the marks of their bondage were never wholly effaced until they were clothed upon with immortality. To those doubting ones earth was a night season of gloom and darkness, and in the border land they saw the dawn of day; and when the summons comes, they are glad to bid farewell to the night that is past, and to welcome with joy and singing, the eternal day, whose sun-rising shall know no sunset.

Mr. Honest.—Thou brave Pilgrim! Jordan this day has overflowed its banks, and its fords are deep, and its swellings high. But thou art strong to breast its waves and to cross its floods! "Good-conscience" is thy succor, and "Grace reigns" thy battle-cry. Pass safely to thy rest! As a brave, manly Pilgrim, "old father HONEST" has fought the good fight, has discomfited many a foe, and by his true faith, and honest walk, and cheerful countenance, he has tended much to mitigate the sorrows and the trials of the Pilgrim-company. These men of generous heart and large experience are as strong pillars, upholding the consistency and strength of the spiritual temple.

Mr. Valiant-for-truth.—Behold, a troop cometh; and now, encompassed with a cloud of witnesses, a trusty Pilgrim adventures the flood! It is VALIANT-FOR-TRUTH that now steps down, and deeper down, and, as he sinks, his voice is lifted up more bravely and more strong, in token that it is Victory still. Death and the grave are overcome in that brief passage; and trumpets sounding at the other side announce that the brave warrior is at rest! His sword, that "right Jerusalem blade," is for all the valiant soldiers of the King— even "the sword of the Spirit, which is the Word of God."*

Mr. Stand-fast.—Last of all, the message comes for STAND-FAST, and he obeys the summons. Here all is calm and peace. No waves or buffetings, no agonies or pains of death. Still and gentle, but yet cold and bitter, are the waters of the river. The dying Pilgrim stands in the midst of the flood, and speaks words of counsel and of ghostly strength to those he leaves behind him. He tells of the goodness of the Lord, and of the joys of his countenance; and how he rejoiced to walk in the footsteps of his Master. Such is the peaceful departure of the steadfast Christian. "Let me die the death of the righteous, and let my last end be like his!"†

The residue of the company are left upon the earth, to pursue their pilgrimage still, to bring forth a people for the Lord, and to await the summons that is yet to call them away, to follow those who have already "through faith and patience inherited the promises." And who next? and next? It may be you, or the summons may be for me! There is something peculiarly solemn, glorious, grand, about this final shadow of the Dreamer's dream, as it thus vanishes from his sight. The finishing touch of the inimitable pencil of the Allegorist shades off the things of earth into the things of heaven, and merges that which is seen, and temporal into that which is unseen and eternal. And thus we bid a reluctant farewell to the

---

*Ephesians 6:17—And take the helmet of salvation, and the sword of the Spirit, which is the word of God.
†Numbers 23:10—Who can count the dust of Jacob, and the number of the fourth part of Israel? Let me die the death of the righteous, and let my last end be like his!

visions of the "Glorious Dreamer," profited by the blest lessons he hath taught us, and encouraged to pursue with greater zeal and vigor the path of our own spiritual pilgrimage to the Better Land.

> "Thither my weak and weary steps are tending—
> Savior and Lord! with Thy frail child abide!
> Guide me toward Home, where, all my wanderings ending,
> I shall see Thee, and shall be satisfied!"

www.ingramcontent.com/pod-product-compliance
Lightning Source LLC
Chambersburg PA
CBHW022114040426
42450CB00006B/694